Wha They Did With Plants

A link with Ireland's Past

This book has received support from the Cultural Traditions Programme of the Community Relations Council which aims to encourage acceptance and understanding of cultural diversity.

Doreen McBride

ADARE PRESS
White Gables
Ballymoney Hill
Banbridge
Telephone: Banbridge 23782

© 1991 Doreen McBride
Published by Adare Press
Typeset by Hallographics, Belfast
Printed by Romac Ltd., Belfast

All rights reserved. No part of this publication may be reproduced, stored in a retrieval system, or transmitted, in any form or by any means, electronic, mechanical, photocopying, recording or otherwise, without the prior permission in writing, of the publisher.

ISBN 0 9516686 1 7

CONTENTS

		Page
Chapter 1	Old Ways with Plants	5
Chapter 2	Linen Cures and Putty from Flax	9
Chapter 3	Furze or Whins	26
Chapter 4	Crab Apples	35
Chapter 5	Mountain Dew	40
Chapter 6	Food, Fertiliser and Things from Seaweed	45
Chapter 7	Potatoes	57
Chapter 8	The Magic of Dye Plants	62
Chapter 9	Plants Used to Cure Disease	67
Chapter 10	What Granny Used To Do	92
Acknowledgements		94
Suggested Reading		95
Index		96

Harold Underwood, 1946.

Chapter 1
OLD WAYS WITH PLANTS

Harold Underwood was old and bent. He had worked as a gardener in Ballievey House near Banbridge, County Down. He was born in 1910. His brown eyes shone and twinkled in his nutbrown face. 'Do you know,' he said, 'that they did very different things with plants in the past compared to what they do today?'
'What do you mean?' I asked.
'Well, in the past people didn't make the same use of artificial fertilisers as they do today. Fertilisers were too expensive, or unobtainable. Farmers stored animal manure, mixed it with straw,

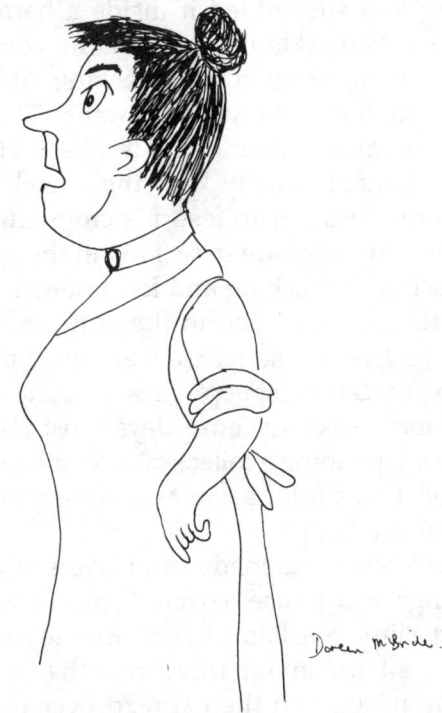

What do you mean? Someone has stolen the manure heap?

allowed it to rot and then spread it on the land. Manure was very precious. It acted as a fertiliser. If land is not fertilised it produces poor crops.

'At the beginning of the last century people stored their manure heaps, called dunghills, in front of the house door so that they could keep an eye on them. There were wicked people around who would steal it.'

I laughed at the idea of anyone stealing a manure heap.

'It was no joke,' scolded Harold, 'If you had your dunghill stolen your family was faced with starvation until you gathered some more together. Remember, in the past many people lived at subsistence level. They had enough for survival if they had a good harvest. If the harvest was poor they went hungry.'

Harold told me that he made a very good liquid fertiliser for his garden by going into a field and lifting a dried cowpat. He placed the dried cow dung inside a piece of sacking, which he had soaked in Copper Sulphate to keep it from rotting. He then tied the sacking with string and suspended it inside a barrel of water, leaving it uncovered outside. He used to stir the contents of the barrel by pulling the string attached to the sacking round and round, trailing it, with its contents, through the water. The cow manure turned the water into an excellent liquid fertiliser. Harold used it to water his crops. Rainfall usually kept the barrel full. Harold obtained enough liquid fertiliser to feed his crops during the summertime by wrapping cow manure in sacking in the spring. He emptied the barrel, placing the sacking and its contents on the compost heap, when he tidied his garden in the autumn.

Animal and vegetable refuse were used to make fertilisers. The droppings of cattle, sheep, pigs and household sewage were collected and saved. In those days most toilets were 'dry' toilets, formed by suspending a toilet seat over a hole in the ground. When the dry toilet was full its contents were dug out and were placed on the manure heap.

A manure heap was made from layers of about 22cm (9 inches) of droppings and refuse, covered, mixed with an equal quantity of soil and a little quicklime to remove the bad smell. The heap was allowed to sit for about three months, was then turned over, thoroughly mixed and then spread over the ground.

William Carleton, in his book 'Traits and Stories of the Irish

Peasantry', Volume II (1868), describes a child playing in a manure heap, as follows:-

'... the floor of his father's house was but a continuation of the dunghill, or the dunghill a continuation of the floor, we know not rightly which, he had a larger scope, and a more unsavoury pool than usual, for amusement. Their dunghill, indeed, was the finest of its size and any kind to be seen; quite a tasteful thing, and so convenient, that he could lay himself down at the hearth, and roll out to its foot, after which he ascended it on his legs, with all the elasticity of a young poet triumphantly climbing Parnassus.'

About 1960 I met an old woman who had a beautiful garden with a fine green lawn. I asked her how she had managed to bring her lawn into such fine condition. She told me that the whole family had chamber pots which they used each night and that she collected their urine each day, placed it in a large bucket added nineteen parts of water to each one part of urine, and used the mixture to water her lawn as a general liquid fertiliser.

There is an old story of two children, a little boy and a little girl, who were each given a part of their garden to tend. The little girl was a very keen gardener. She loved her little patch and spent hours tenderly caring for it, keeping it weeded and she fed her plants with liquid manure. The little boy started off each Spring with a rush of enthusiasm. He dug the ground and planted radishes, then he tended to forget, so that his patch became covered in weeds. Nobody could explain why his radishes were so much better than those of his sister until one day she remarked 'Mummy — I do wish I had a thing built into me to water my garden the way James does.'

Sheila Harrington lives in Bantry, County Cork. She has a small, carefully tended garden. Sheila believed that the soil was becoming exhausted because over the years the size of the onions she produced had become smaller and smaller. An old gardener described how he had grown onions in the past. He told her that each spring he had collected a bucketful of nettles, added water to the bucket so that the nettles were submerged, left them for between four and six weeks to allow fermentation to take place, then used the mixture to water his onions. Sheila followed his instructions and the quality and quantity of the onions she produced improved enormously.

Today there is a lot of concern about the levels of nitrates from fertiliser which have seeped into drinking water, and the possibility of cancers being caused by crops sprayed with insecticides and weed killers. Perhaps it would be a good idea to adapt some of the customs of the past to the present.

In the past dandelions were not treated with weed killer. Instead, the tops were cut off and a pinch of salt was placed on the wound; aphids were brushed off plants with an aphid brush, earwigs were caught in simple traps. Earwigs like to squeeze into small spaces so an upturned flower pot was filled with crumpled paper, or straw, and placed on top of a cane. During the night the hollow cane attracted the earwig to climb up into the pot. Once inside the pot it snuggled up and prepared to spend the day there. These earwigs were then killed by shaking the pot during the day time, causing them to fall onto the ground where they were flattened and killed by the judicious use of a foot! Ernest Scott remembers destroying wasps nests by pouring boiling water over them, then running away as fast as his legs would carry him!

Not all methods of killing pests in the past were harmless. Ants were killed by pouring boiling water, or a mixture of sugar and beer in which arsenic had been mixed, over the nest. Arsenic was a common chemical in the past. It was freely available and could be bought, without any type of restriction, in spirit grocers. Ladies used it as a beauty aid because it gave them pale complexions. People did not realise how dangerous it was.

Chapter 2
LINEN, CURES AND PUTTY FROM FLAX

I have childhood memories of being driven in my father's car through Ireland's beautiful countryside on lovely August days. I was always filled with pleasure as I admired the scenery and enjoyed the sun, then sometimes, during late summer, I became aware of the the most ghastly smell, a revolting stench which made me feel sick.

Ugh! 'Mummy,' I asked for the umpeenth time, as I found the answer difficult to believe, 'what is that terrible smell?'

'Child dear,' she replied, 'They have opened a flax dam and are lifting the flax out to make Irish linen.' I could not understand how such a horrible smell could ever be part of the process of making fine, white, Irish linen

Linen fibres are formed inside flax plants.

Flax plants are similar to all other flowering plants. They have a root to anchor them to the soil and bring water inside, leaves which make plant food and flowers which produce seeds. The stem passes water and mineral salts up the plant and food from the leaves up and down inside the plant to where it is needed. Inside the stem there are tubes, called 'phloem tubes', which are used to pass plant food up and down the plant. Flax plants have unusually strong phloem tubes; they can be made into linen threads.

Flax has been grown in Ireland for a long time. It is mentioned in literature of the early Christian period when it was made into linen to make vestments for the clerics.

Until the early part of the eighteenth century most small farms produced a little flax. Farmers sowed some flax, then dressed, spun and wove it into linen for their own use. If they had any yarn left over, it was sold.

During the last three hundred years growing flax has been linked to large scale commercial production of linen. More flax was grown in Ulster than in any of the other Provinces in Ireland, but there is very little grown today.

Flax was known to be a 'greedy crop'. It took a lot of nourishment out of the soil and was usually grown in a 'plant succession' after potatoes, where the ground had had a lot of manure added to it to make sure of a good potato crop.

Two varieties of flax were grown, one with blue flowers, the other with white. The blue flowered variety was the most common except, in the Braid Valley near Ballymena. In this region the blue flowered variety tended to be attacked by rust disease. The white flowered variety was more rust resistant so it was grown there.

The ground was prepared very carefully for flax crops. It was often ploughed three or more times to obtain a sufficiently fine tilth. The first time the land was ploughed the weeds were buried, but the tilth was probably not fine enough. The second ploughing improved the state of the soil but brought the weeds back up to the surface.

Flax seeds were sown broadcast.

The third ploughing buried the weeds again and gave the fine tilth needed.

Flax seed was usually sown broadcast. If it was sown in drills there tended to be a relatively wide space at each side of the plant. This wide space encouraged short side stems to grow and fibre in side stems was of limited value. Flax seeds are difficult to sow evenly because they are shiny and tend to slip too easily out of the hand. They are small, light and easily blown by a breeze.

Well prepared ground was usually relatively free from weeds, but the crop was weeded when it was about about nine centimetres, (four inches) high. During the eighteenth and early nineteenth centuries it was weeded by women and children. They crawled over the earth on their hands and knees, pulling weeds out, taking care not to disturb the plant roots. The weeders flattened the crop as they crawled on top of it. The plants recovered quickly provided they were less than fourteen centimetres (about six inches) in height, when they became too brittle to straighten up again.

Flax was ready to be harvested about fourteen weeks after it was sown, that is, about three or four weeks after the first blossoms appeared.

Farmers needed a great deal of expertise to help decide exactly when the flax should be harvested. If the crop was pulled too soon the fibres were soft and weak, resulting in a low yield. Flax for the finest linen was harvested earliest. If the crop was left too long only coarse linen could be made from it because the fibres became too thick to make fine linen.

Flax was harvested by being pulled out by the roots. The phloem tubes which form the linen threads begin in the root, so cutting the stalks wasted good fibre. Until the 1940s flax grown for linen was pulled by hand. Harvesters grasped the flax about halfway up the plant stems. They pulled upwards and slightly to one side. Four handfuls of flax made a 'beet' or sheaf. The beets were tied, usually by bands made of rushes. They were destined to lie rotting under water for approximately two weeks. Rushes do not rot under water while string and rope do.

Once the flax was pulled the immature seeds had to be removed. This was done by a process known as 'rippling'. The beets were pulled through a structure called a 'rippling comb'. The rippling comb was made from a plank which was supported above the

Pulling flax, Ulster Folk and Transport Museum, August 1990.

A beet of flax, Ulster Folk and Transport Museum, August 1990.

ground and had a set of 25 cm (10 inch) iron teeth driven into it. The rippling comb was sometimes placed in the back of a cart so that the seed fell into the cart when it was knocked off the plants. Seed was used to feed animals or to make linseed oil. It was not possible to produce good linen and a good harvest of seeds. The seed heads were still immature when the linen threads were ready to be harvested.

Seedless beets were put into flax dams. Another name for flax dam was lint hole. A typical dam in Ulster measured 26m by 2.5m (70 feet by 7 feet). It was narrow so that workers could 'fork' beets, that is, use an agricultural fork to throw the beets, from both sides of the dam into the water. The water was about one metre (three and a half feet) in depth. It was warmest at the top and coldest at the bottom. If the water was any deeper than three and a half feet it proved too cold to allow easy retting.

Retting was usually started before the middle of August to make sure that the water was sufficiently warm. During retting the

The flax beets were pulled through a rippling comb.

flax plant decayed so that the phloem tubes, which could be turned into linen threads, could be separated.

Beets destined to make fine linen were placed at the bottom of the dam while coarse beets were placed at the top because they retted more easily and could be removed sooner. The beets were weighted down by large stones.

John Campbell remembers flax dams in County Armagh near Mullaghbawn, along the road where he walked with his brother on their way home from school. According to John, the water in which flax was retting became covered in foam which looked like soap bubbles. The two small boys loved to jump into the dams and leap up and down on top of the stones. The water did not feel cold and small boys found the bouncy sensation delightful! Farmers did not object to this type of activity because it stirred the water and made the retting process quicker. John says that once the water had been well and truly stirred it was possible to obtain an interesting blue flame by lighting a match and holding it just above the surface. The flame shot over the surface, looking for all the world like the flame on a Christmas pudding which had been covered in brandy and set alight.

The time flax beets were kept in the flax dam depended on the weather, the quality of the water and the type of flax.

Flax dams were usually dug near a water supply, such as a lake or stream, so that they could be filled easily. The water in which flax had been steeped was highly poisonous to fish and it stank. When the flax was retted and had been removed, farmers were advised to let the dam empty itself by seepage, or to let it into a stream which was in full flood, to minimise the effects of pollution.

Lifting the beets out of the water was a most unpleasant job. The workers had to climb into the stinking water and lift them out by hand. The workers became covered in a disgusting smelly slime which clung to their skin and was difficult to remove. The womenfolk of men who had been submerged in flax water, complained that their men stank for days afterwards. Unmarried men with girl friends were very reluctant to lift the beets out of a dam! As a result, most of the beets were lifted out by married men who were thought to be past the age of romance, or by teenage boys who thought women were a waste of time!

Obviously, flax which had just been removed from the dam was

No — I won't get into the dam. It'd spoil my chances of romance.

saturated with water and needed to be dried. One of two methods was used for drying. The beets could be taken from the dam and set upright to drain, then, after a few hours, carted to a field and spread out in rows to dry. The flax was turned several times, as it dried, to prevent discolouration. In fine weather the drying was complete within six days, but if the weather was unsuitable, drying could take up to two weeks.

Some Ulster farmers used a method of drying flax which was similar to haymaking. They waited until the flax was almost dry, then 'gaited' it! 'Gaitin' were made. Each gaitin was formed in the same way as a beet. A large handful of flax was picked up so that all the roots were together. It was then tied nearer the top than a beet. The bottom of the plant stems were spread out forming a wide base on which the gaitin stood. The gaitins were left standing for anything between two days and a week, when they were made into a rick. The field could not be used for any other purpose during the time the gaitins were drying.

Ernest Scott remembers another, more economical way of drying flax. Branches were cut out of hedges and stuck into the ground, twine was tied between the branches forming a type of fence. The gaitins were hung up to dry on the twine. Gaitins dried by this method were ready within a few hours to be formed into ricks and the field was free for other uses.

Flax was built into structures which could be up to 10 metres (thirty feet) in length. The flax was stored in ricks, or made into structures, called hovels, sleighs or rays, until it was the farmer's turn to go to the scutch mill.

According to Ernest Scott, there was an old saying 'Short accounts mean long friends.' If accounts were settled promptly with scutch mill owners, the following year the time one was kept waiting for scutching was kept to a minimum!

Ronnie Patton remembers building hovels as a youth. Each hovel contained one hundred or more gaitins built into two storeys. The first storey consisted of three rows of gaitins on each side with a row of gaitins along the eaves, like building a house. The hovel was built up thus and finally thatched with rushes, whins or any other material which was plentiful locally. The complete structure was rain and storm proof and the wind was able to blow through it thus drying the flax.

During scutching the unwanted dried parts of the plant were knocked off the linen fibres. This was normally done in a scutch mill. To begin with, flax entering a scutch mill was 'bruised' by being run through wooden rollers. Bruising loosened the unwanted plant parts and made the stiff, dried plants pliable. The flax was then taken over to an upright, wooden post, or 'stock' and hit with a blunt wooden blade. This knocked the unwanted plant parts off the fibre and produced threads which could be spun and then woven into linen.

Scutch mills were horrible places in which to work. They were dark and the air was clouded with dust from the flax plants. The dust was highly flammable so that the mills frequently caught fire and burnt down. The scutch mill which has been rebuilt in the Ulster Folk and Transport Museum originally came from Gorticashel in County Armagh. It suffered extensive fire damage during its working history.

Dust from the flax got into the workers' lungs and aggravated any tendency to suffer from asthma, bronchitis or other lung diseases. Workers who lost concentration for a few seconds could be caught by the machinery and mutilated. The 'Down Recorder', Saturday 18th. November 1893 has a report of an accident that happened to an elderly, crippled woman, called Annie Mulligan. The scutching machinery in David McMordie's at Drumaughis, near Crossgar, County Down, was working and Annie was taking her place sitting beside it, when she fell. Her hands landed on the teethed rollers and were pulled off. Before help could arrive the right side of her body was dreadfuly mangled and her scalp was torn off. The mill owner stopped the machinery as soon as was humanly possible, but it was too late for Annie. The unfortunate woman was picked out of the machinery in pieces.

My father, William Henry, worked for the Ocean Insurance Company during the the Second World War. He was responsible for accident insurance and insured the owners of scutch mills. According to him scutch mills were so dangerous that a directive came from the head office of the Ocean Insurance Company in London saying that the Company could no longer handle insurance of scutch mills because it was making heavy losses. Dad thought that was ridiculous. He felt it was wrong to sell accident insurance only to people who did not need it! He believed that the risks could be assessed, a reasonable premium charged and a profitable business organised. He inspected scutch mills throughout Northern Ireland, suggested a few modifications in design, where needed, such as making the tables in front of the machinery wider so that mill workers could not accidently lean over and become caught. The Ocean Insurance Company listened to him, reorganised and continued to insure scutch mills until they disappeared.

When scutching was complete the linen fibres were ready to be spun into linen threads. First of all they were 'hackled' by being pulled through a 'hackling comb'. This made sure that the fibres were all lying the same way. Spinning bends and twists comparatively short fibres into a long yarn. Before industrialisation women worked at home with spinning wheels.

The 'chowes', that is the waste left over from scutching, were collected by the poor and used as stuffing for such things as mattresses.

The spun threads were wound into 'hanks' which were boiled before being woven into cloth.

Nora Bates, who lives in Antrim, remembers working in the flax rooms of Comber Mill, which was owned by John Andrews, during the 1940s. She says that the rooms where she worked were large, the air was dry and full of dust. The nature of the task meant that the windows could not be opened. Nora felt ill most of the time she worked there. If she was not employed in a dusty room she was sent to work in one of the rooms where she had to stand in water all day. Norah says she was a 'spreader' when she began to work in the mill. The flax fibres came along a conveyor belt. Norah made sure they were straight. The flax fibres disappeared into a tunnel at the end of the room.

I remember, during the 1950s, travelling into Belfast on the 'Castlereagh' bus to school each day. I saw women mill workers rushing to work. Many of these women had no shoes on their feet. On frosty days their bare feet appeared blue with the cold. They wore no coats but wrapped heavy shawls, or rugs around their shoulders to keep the cold out, looking sodden and miserable on days in which the rain came down in what was described locally as 'stair-rods.'

The cloth was woven on a loom. First of all the horizontal threads were fixed into position. They were stretched tightly between the beams at the front and the back of the loom. The beam at the back of the loom was called the warp boom while that at the front was known as the cloth beam. Weavers made a shed which lifted and lowered alternative sets of threads. This allowed a shuttle carrying a thread, called the weft thread, to be passed through the shed, the weft threads being pushed tight against each other by a comb-like structure called a reed.

Linen straight from the loom was a dark, dull, brown colour which needed to be bleached to make it white. The linen was spread out on the bleaching green until the action of the sun turned it white. Linen bleaching in the sun was very valuable. Watch towers were built beside bleaching greens and men were hired to shelter inside the watch towers to prevent the linen being stolen, or damaged by straying animals such as cows.

The penalties for stealing linen were very severe. Starving wretches who stole linen in an attempt to raise some cash to buy

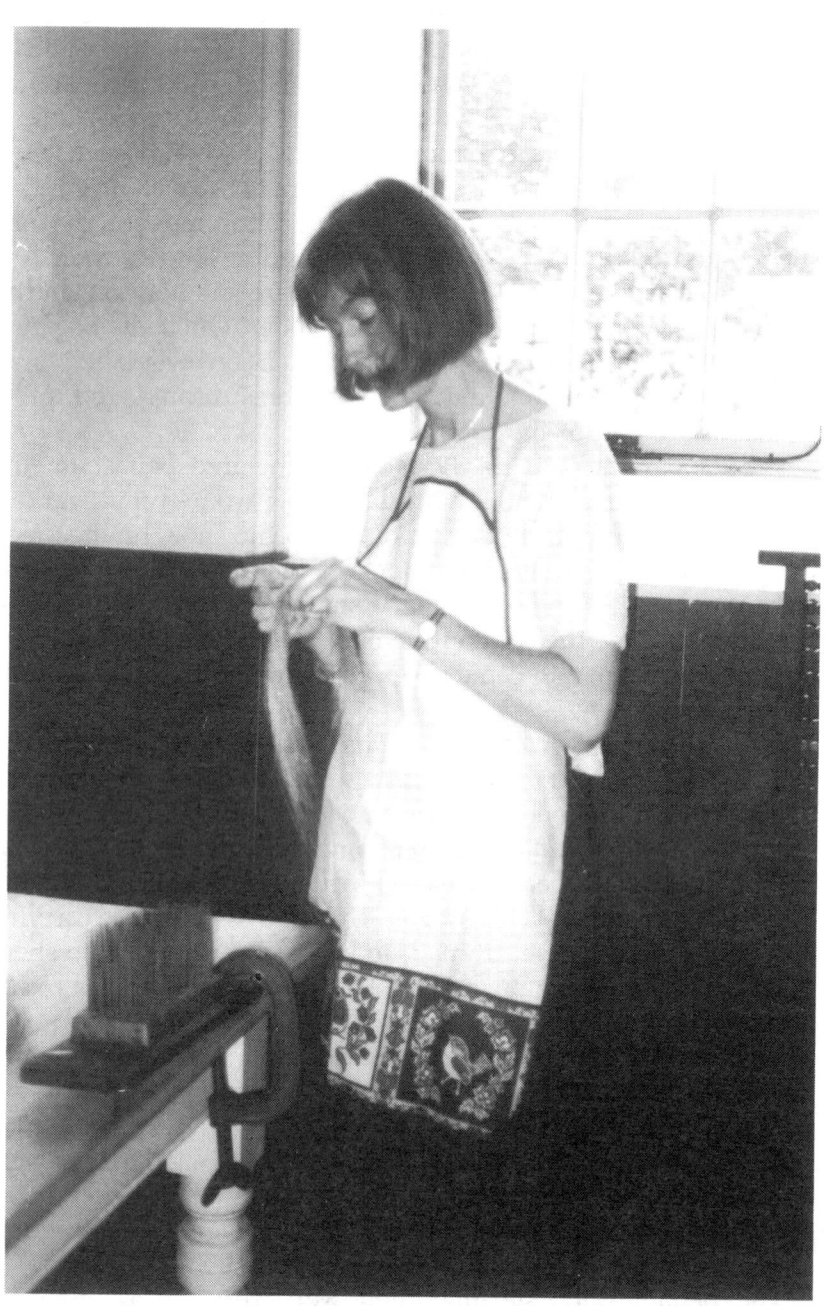
Hackling linen threads, Ulster Folk and Transport Museum.

Spinning, Ulster Folk and Transport Museum, August 1990.

food for their families could be punished. If they were lucky, they had a hand cut off. Stiffer sentences included hanging and deportation! The 'Belfast News Letter', 11th April 1783 reports on convictions for robbing bleach greens. The following people were found guilty, and received sentences as follows, — 'Patrick Gordon, otherwise McGurnahan (to be executed at Drumbridge on Thursday next the 17th inst.) and Stephen Gordon, otherwise McGurnaghan (to be executed at Castlewellan on Monday next the 14th inst.) for stealing linen out of the bleach green of George and Walter Crawford of Ballievey.'

Very little flax is grown in Ireland today. There still is a linen industry, although it is a shadow of its former self. Today imported linen, coming mainly from Belgium, is used. Most of the old linen mills have been demolished or lie decaying, although some have been adapted for new functions like the old linen mill at Tullylish,

Linen from the loom was brown in colour. It was spread out on grass areas, called bleaching greens to be bleached white by the sun.

Weaving on table top loom, Ulster Folk and Transport Museum, 1990.

County Down, which has been converted into a restaurant with a Pottery attached. Pots made in Tullylish Pottery are exported throughout the world, so, in a strange way, the export tradition begun by the old linen mill is being continued.

The Fashion Centre for Northern Ireland in Ormeau Avenue, Belfast, which provides a place where local talented designers can show their wares, is a converted linen mill.

A few of the old mills, such as Kirkpatrick Linron (Ballyclare) Ltd., have managed to survive by changing their products and evolving with the times. This firm has stopped finishing cloths and now concentrates on producing fibre, called 'linron', which enables linen fibres to be blended with other types of fibre. The linron is bleached and dyed, then sold to be spun into thread. This enterprising company has been in existence for more than two hundred and fifty years.

Flax seeds were used to make linseed oil. If flax seeds are pressed when they are cold, an edible, almost colourless oil, comes out. This oil was used to soften and break abscesses and tumours, to take away spots and freckles and, when mixed with equal parts of lime water, it was called 'Carron oil' and used to treat burns.

Constipation was cured by drinking an infusion of linseed, which also reduced inflammation of the mouth and throat.

If the flax seeds were pressed when they were hot then a yellowish-brown oil, with a peculiar smell and taste, was produced. This oil became solid when exposed to the air for some hours and was used as a varnish. The oil formed a better varnish if it was heated for several hours.

Linseed oil was used to make paints, printing ink and linoleum. Linoleum, sometimes called 'lino', was a very useful, hard-wearing, type of floor covering, formed from a type of jute hessian cloth covered by layers of oxidised linseed oil and other oily resinous substances mixed with ground cork.

Putty, used for holding glass in windows, was made from linseed oil mixed with powdered limestone known as whiting. The best quality whiting came from the Antrim Coast.

According to Graham Millar, a putty manufacturer, it is possible to make small amounts of putty in a container such as a basin, a bucket, or a large bowl, simply by mixing the linseed oil with the whiting. Putty making is an art and judging its consistency is difficult. It must remain pliable in the glazier's hands as he works yet be sufficiently firm to hold the glass in place. An expert putty maker judges if the putty is of the correct consistency by feeling it with his fingers.

Graham says that an old farmer in County Antrim told him that he used to make putty in the past by placing linseed oil and whiting in an old zinc bath and mixing it with his feet, somewhat in the fashion of winemakers treading grapes.

Putty is manufactured in putty mills which are simply large containers used to mix the linseed oil and whiting. The introduction of plastic and of aluminium windows has caused a decline in putty manufacture.

Linen, linseed oil, ink, floor covering, country cures and putty, the number of uses found for a simple, unprepossessing little plant is amazing, and I do love the traditional rhyme:

> *"Excuse me Miss for grinning,*
> *I see something tnat needs pinning.*
> *There's a little bit of linen hanging down."*

Chapter 3
FURZE OR WHINS

There is an old saying:-

'Gold under the Furze,
Silver under the grass,
Hunger under the heather'.

It means that rich soil is found under furze, reasonable soil under grass and very poor quality soil under heather, which will produce poor crops, resulting in hunger.

What is furze? In different parts of the country the same plant may be called by different names. This is true of the furze which is called 'gorse' in England. In Ireland 'gorse' is called 'furze' south of a line drawn roughly east to west across the country from the neighbourhood of Drogheda in County Louth to Westport in County Mayo and 'whins' north of the line. I live north of this line so I am going to refer to the plant as 'whins'.

Whins are able to make the soil richer because they have nodules on their roots which act as home to a very special type of bacteria. These bacteria can trap nitrogen from the air so that the whins are, in effect, able to make their own fertiliser.

Whin plants are covered with dark green spines which keep animals from eating them, so they can be used as hedging. These spines developed from modified leaves and shoots. Plants with leaves developed into spines have a big advantage. They do not lose as much water as plants with normal leaves and so they are able to live in dry, shallow soils in windy conditions which would kill normal plants.

Leaves are plants' food-producing factories. Plants make food by using energy from the sun, the green chemical called chlorophyll and carbon dioxide gas from the air. Plants whose leaves turn into spines have one big disadvantage. Fewer leaves mean less chlorophyll and a reduced food supply. Whins are unusual in that they have chlorophyll in the spines so compensating for leaf loss. Whins are very hardy and can survive in very difficult conditions.

Whins were used for hedging and to feed cows, sheep, goats and horses when fresh grass, or hay, was in short supply. Horses' coats became glossy when they were fed on whins. The whins appear to have the same effect on horses as garlic does on humans! A horse which had not been fed on whins would refuse to work with one which was. It was believed that the breath of the whin-fed horse would take the strength of the other. The remedy was quite simple — make sure both horses had a feed of whins!

There were several ways of using whins as animal fodder. The tender shoots were mashed and served, or lumps were cut out of the bushes, using a sickle and a forked stick, and either chopped up finely or pounded on a large, flat stone to destroy the prickles. Some houses had a trough dug into the floor of the kitchen, usually

Using a flat stone to prepare whins as fodder.

near the door, in which the whins were prepared as fodder. This meant that the person doing the work was protected from the weather.

Records exist* which show that during the winter months cows ate whins, potato skins, and the water in which potatoes had been boiled. Cows frequently died of the disease known as 'big gall' when they went out to grass following the winter during which they had been fed on whins, straw or potatoes. When a cow suffered from 'big gall' it became swollen because gas became trapped inside its digestive system. According to Ernest Scott, in the old days the gas was released by measuring one hand span up from the hip bone and sticking a knife into the animal's flank. This released the gas trapped inside the unfortunate animal and saved its life. Ernest says it was possible to set the escaping gas alight. Today vets release gas trapped inside cows by inserting a tube through the cow's mouth

*Wakefield, Edward. An Account of Ireland Statistical and Political. London 1812, vol. 1, p. 390.

Using a chopper in a sunken trough to prepare whins as fodder.

I absolutely refuse to get up and go to work unless you go and cut some whins for my bed.

and into its stomach. The problem can be avoided by leaving a bale of straw out in the field which the cows will eat if they feel their food is too rich and beginning to cause internal problems!

Surprisingly enough, animal bedding was made from whins. One would have thought that such a prickly plant would have been unsuitable for bedding. It was used by being spread in a thick layer over the shed in which the animals were housed. The layer, which could be several feet thick, was firmed down by trampling, then covered by a layer of straw, or other soft litter. Whins make an excellent bedding material because they stay warm and dry. The open texture traps air which insulates the animal against the cold floor and allows urine to drain off so that the upper, soft layer does not become sodden.

Whins which had been used for bedding were placed on the dung heap to add to the farm's fertiliser supply.

During the winter months farm yards tended to become very wet so that anyone walking across became covered in mud, also called 'clabber' in Ireland. Rainwater collected in puddles and mixed with urine and animal droppings making a ghastly mess. Farmers cut large amounts of whins and spread them around the farmyard, in front of the byre and stable doors, on lanes and passageways leading from the yard to the fields and in any other places which had animals frequently walking across them. In the past cows spending the winter sheltered from bad weather in byres had to be let out twice a day to drink from a stream. Each cow needs twenty gallons to enable it to produce about five gallons of milk. It was impossible, because of the time involved, to carry that amount before water was piped into byres.

The animals trampled upon the whins and enriched them with their droppings. They were broken down by the wheels of carts and other farm traffic. Eventually they were scraped up, added to the dung heap, allowed to rot further and used as a manure.

Whins were used on their own as a manure, if animal droppings were not available. They were spread out on the ground and then covered with a layer of soil in which crops were planted.

Strangely enough, whins were also used to roof houses. Small sticks cut from whins were built into roofs and used as a foundation for thatch. Sometimes whins were used for thatching and at times to make animal shelters in fields away from the farmstead. A U-shaped fence was made of two vertical walls of netting wire about 15 cm (one foot) apart. Whins were packed into the space. As the whins withered they sank and fresh supplies were laid on top. These rough shelters were often thatched with whins weighted down with large stones, to keep them from blowing away.

In the more distant past whins were used as a bonding material when making mud walls, although chopped straw or rushes were more common for this purpose. They were used in a similar way by old fashioned masons up to the beginning of the twentieth century, as a bond for lime and sand plaster. The plaster stuck to the wall better if finely chopped whins were added to it.

In the past there was no barbed wire, no netting wire, no chain-link fencing and no electric fences so whins acted as fencing. They have very dense, spreading tops with masses of prickles which spread out in all directions. The prickles remain attached to the plant long after it is dead and withered. A hay rope interlaced with whins formed a primitive type of barbed wire. Whins where used to stop holes in all types of fence. Gates, leading to gardens and fields with crops which could be damaged by fowl, were laced with whin bushes to keep the fowl out.

Whin bushes were used to clean chimneys. Most of traditional houses in Ireland were low, single storey structures and the total length of the chimney was not great. Chimneys were wide at the bottom, to collect the smoke from the open hearth, and became narrower towards the roof. Whins formed an excellent brush because they were yielding enough to be manoeuvred easily, yet stiff enough to scour the chimney surface, and close set enough to be able to sweep the maximum surface with the minimum effort. It was possible to make a brush of exactly the right size for a particular chimney by taking a whole bush and trimming it. Sometimes a number of branches were tied together to make a brush and occasionally a double-headed brush was formed by tying the stems of two bushes together so that the bushy tops were at opposite ends.

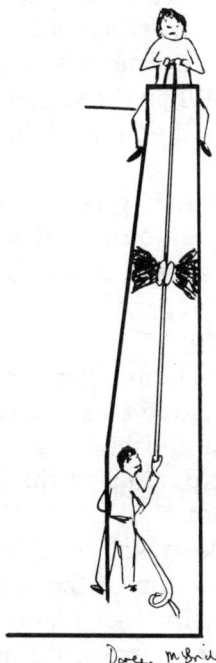

How whins were used to clean chimneys.

The bush was used as a brush by tying it on a stick and pushing it up and down the chimney. A more efficient way of cleaning the chimney was to tie the bush in the middle of a piece of rope. One man climbed on top of the roof and dropped an end of the rope down the chimney which was caught by the other man. The men then pulled the bush up and down inside the chimney breast like a seasaw.

Whins were tied together and set into shafts forming a broom called a besom.

Whins had other uses, including the foundation of roads through boggy country and as field drains before the introduction of pipes. There were two ways of using whins in drains. Either, a trench was dug and two continuous lines of flat stones were set along the bottom with their edges leaning against each other so that they formed a channel with a triangular cross section. Stones were placed on top of the sloping stones and up the sides of the trench. A layer of whins was placed on top of the stones to keep soil from being washed down through them. Sometimes whins were placed directly on top of the bottom stones. Or, a trench was dug down into the sub-soil, green whins where placed in it and walked on until they were well tramped down. The clay subsoil was then replaced, followed by the top soil. When the whins decayed they left a tunnel because the clay set above them. Such drains could remain effective for more than fifty years.

Whin flowers were used to give a yellow dye. In the past few people had scales so the amount of flowers needed was a matter of experience combined with guess work. The flowers are stronger in the summer than they are in the winter because there is more sap in them.

Whin flowers were placed in a pot, covered in water and boiled to make a dye. When the water turned yellow the substance to be dyed was put in the pot and boiled along with the flowers. The boiling process took the dye out of the flowers. Salt and vinegar were used to make it fast.

Whins were used to clean wells and harrow soil. When a whin bush was drawn over the top of the water it collected debris. A bundle of whins tied together, weighted by a stone and pulled by a horse, made an efficient harrow. Whins were used as steading for stacks. They kept vermin out and allowed air to circulate so that plants stored in a stack did not rot. The white ash of whins was used as a scouring agent.

Whins were, within living memory, used as a fuel in Mourne Bakeries. Whins gave intense heat and little ash.

Whins were used as country cures. People sucked the bark, or ate the soft young tops to cure heartburn.

Whin flowers were stewed in water for several hours, the liquid strained off, bottled and taken as a tonic.

A handful of whin blossoms was put in a cupful of milk and boiled. The mixture was strained, cooled and given to children to drink first thing in the morning when their stomachs were empty, to cure worms. In the past worms were a real problem, as far as children were concerned, because they were so easily caught from farm animals. People had a horror of children suffering from worms.

When I was very young my mother used to worm my sister and me every Saturday. We used to dread Saturdays! Life was not full of fun. We went to school during the week and were wormed on Saturdays! We lived in the middle of Belfast, far away from a supply of whins, so Mum bought senna pods and boiled them in water to make a revolting tea which we were forced to drink. It was absolutely ghastly and made us feel sick. Then we spent a couple of hours suffering from diarrhoea.

Mum spent a lot of her childhood living with her aunts on a farm near Ballynure. She said that she was wormed once a week when she was a child and she felt that worming was a necessary part of child rearing.

A more pleasant use of whin flowers was to make wine.

WHIN FLOWER WINE

2 litres (½ gallon) whin flowers
4 ½ litres (8 pints) water
1-1½ kg (2½-3 lb) sugar
1 tablespoon cold tea
1 orange
1 lemon
50g (2 oz) root ginger (optional)
25g (1 oz) yeast
Place the water in a large sauce-pan.
Add the ginger, the juice of the fruit and the rind (without the pith).

Place the whin flowers in a muslin bag and put into the water.
Simmer for about 15 minutes.
Remove the flowers and throw away.
Leave for 5 days, stirring occasionally.
Strain into a fermentation jar.
Dissolve the sugar in hot water.
Allow to cool, add cold tea and yeast.
Add dissolved sugar, cold tea and yeast mixture to fermentation jar.
Ferment to finish.
Bottle wine and leave to mature.

It is difficult to think of any plant which had more uses than whins. They are still in use as hedging and as jumps, commonly known as hurles, in point to point horse races.

I have heard The Kingdom of Mourne referred to as 'the place they found the whins'.

There are many hills throughout Ireland known as 'Whinny Hill' or 'Whinny Brae' and many 'Whinstone Roads'. It is not surprising the whins were taken abroad by settlers from Ireland. They were so useful. Unfortunately whins taken to New Zealand bred with the wild enthuasism shown by rabbits in Australia. Whole mountainsides in New Zealand cringe under attack by whins and fortunes are spent each year trying to eradicate it.

There is an old saying:- 'Never kiss a girl unless the whins are in bloom.' If the country is examined sufficiently thoroughly it is always possible to find some whins blooming somewhere!

Chapter 4
CRAB APPLES

Crab apple trees have been associated with fairies. Many places, such as the 'Fairy River' near Omagh, are named because in the past crab apple trees grew there.

According to ancient Irish folklore magic apple trees grew on the Celtic Isles of the Blest. They had beautiful blossoms that yielded single fruits. Anyone eating one of these fruits was guaranteed to live for at least one hundred years. Hence the old saying 'An apple a day keeps the doctor away.'

On the Isles of the Blest, fairy maidens seduced men by offering them apples. Seduction by a fairy led literally to a fate worse than death. The poor man wasted away and died young although he was often inspired to write great poetry. His soul could never rest as it was cursed and condemmed to haunt the countryside for ever, a miserable wandering ghost.

Crab apple trees are native to Ireland. As a rule the apples are small, round and bright green or yellow. Some have a scarlet flush. There is an old folk tale that explains why rosy red apples are often found in County Armagh. Bailie, heir to the throne of Ulster, fell in love with Aillin, daughter of the King of Leinster. This was a terrible thing. Even in those legendary time there was trouble between North and South. Both sets of parents objected very strongly to the match. They thought it could start a war between the two Provinces. The young people refused to pay any attention to their parents and continued to meet secretly. Eventually the Druids were consulted. They arrived at a strange conclusion. The lovers could not be together in this world but could in eternity.

Bailie and Aillin made plans for a secret meeting at Rossnaree on the banks of the River Boyne. Bailie set off quietly and reached Dundalk. He rested on the beach when news reached him of Aillin's death. He died of grief. A similar story was told to Aillin who also died of a broken heart. According to tradition an apple and a yew tree were planted on the graves and the apple had a red flush similar to the one that stained Aillin's cheeks when Bailie first told her of his love.

Dundalk's old name, Trough Bailie, was after Bailie. More than a hundred years after Bailie's death the greatest figure in the Ulster Cycle of Stories, Setanta, was born at the ancient fortress, Dun Dealgan, which dominated the town and the name changed. Dundalk is a corruption of Dun Dealgan.

According to tradition, apples were saved for St. Brigid's Eve, that is, the last night in January. An old fashioned griddle apple-cake formed part of the feast which followed the practice of making St. Brigid Crosses. Sometimes apple dumplings were made on St. Brigid's Eve, although they were more common at Hallowe'en, when they were often flavoured with whiskey. Sometimes the apples were

No thank you Aggie, I'll not have an apple in case you are a fairy and I turn into a poet.

Ah — well — A wet St. Swithin's Day gives a good crop of large apples.

roasted, sweetened with sugar, flavoured with nutmeg and served with a whiskey sauce.

    Old superstition says that a wet St. Swithin's Day indicates a really good crop of large apples. Another old belief is that a tree bearing fruit and blossom at harvest time means that there will be a death in the family before the next harvest.

In the past apples were used to treat ulcerated wounds. The woodland plant, sorrel was crushed and mixed with apple juice and placed on the wound. Crab apples were also used to make poultices, and used to make verjuice, known as cider vinegar, as well as wine and jelly. Some cider was made although the tradition is not as strong as it is in England.

VERJUICE (Cider Vinegar)

Verjuice is really a slightly fermented cider. It has a very sharp taste. Crab apples do not need to be peeled or cored so windfalls may be used.

The crab apples should be left on the tree for as long as possible without risking exposure to severe frost. Once gathered they should be placed in a pile in a cold, dark room until they begin to sweat. Then the bad fruit should be removed and the remainder crushed in an apple press. The juice should be collected and bottled and left in a cool place for some weeks before being used.

CRAB APPLE JELLY

Crab apple jelly is probably the best jelly of all.
500g (1lb) crab apples
Sugar
Water
Chop the apples into quarters (do not core or peel).
Cover with water and cook until pulpy.
Strain overnight through a jelly bag.
Measure the juice and add 500g (1 lb) of warmed sugar for each ½ litre (pint) of juice.
Boil rapidly for about forty minutes until the jelly sets when tested.
(Test by putting a teaspoon of jelly on a cool plate.
Blow on the jelly on the plate. If a skin forms on it it is ready.)
Place jelly in warmed jam-jars, allow to cool and cover.

Crab apple jelly may be flavoured with a clove, or with cinnamon. The juice of a lemon is another pleasant flavour which may be added.

CRAB APPLE AND BLACKBERRY JELLY

Add 1kg (2 lbs) of blackberries to the above recipe.

CRAB APPLE AND ROSE HIP JELLY

Make as for crab apple jelly but use 1½ kg (3 lbs) apples and 500 g (1 lb) rose hips.

APPLE AND BLACKBERRY MOUSSE

500g (1 lb) crab apples
Juice of 1 lemon
500g (1lb) blackberries
Whites of 2 eggs
125g (4 oz) sugar
½ cup water
Tablespoon gelatine
Sprinkle the gelatine on the juice of a lemon and leave to one side.
Peel, core and slice the crab apples.
Wash the blackberries.
Place the apples and blackberries in a saucepan with the water.
Add 75g (3oz) sugar, cover with a lid and simmer until the fruit is soft (about 15 minutes).
Remove saucepan and allow to cool slightly.
Stir in the lemon juice and gelatine.
Make sure it is thoroughly mixed.
Put the mixture through a sieve.
(A liquidiser is very useful and achieves the same end product!).
Allow to cool and begin to thicken.
Whisk the egg whites until stiff then fold in the remaining sugar 25g (1 oz).
Fold into the fruit and leave in a cold place.

There was a tradition which I always enjoyed when I was a child. Each Spring people climbed into their cars and went for a drive through the apple country in County Armagh. There is no more beautiful sight than that of apple blossoms against a clear blue sky. In County Armagh cultivated apples thrive in the orchards while crabs abound in the hedgerows. Truly apples have been blessed!

Chapter 5
MOUNTAIN DEW

Mountain dew, whiskey, poteen, 'the cratur', call it what you will, it has entered the realms of legend in Ireland.

To begin with it is illegal. The forces of the law searched the countryside impounding stills and punishing their owners.

Pat Cassidy remembers the days when poteen was made in County Fermanagh.

Poteen was originally made from germinated barley. That made the best whiskey of all, but it proved to be very dangerous for the maker. The barley needed to be spread out and dried and it needed space to germinate. The amount of space required meant that several people knew that poteen manufacture was taking place. There was the resultant danger of a security leak to the forces of the law. A change in manufacturing was obviously required so people turned to making poteen out of water, sugar and yeast. These three substances are normally found in every household so it was impossible to arrest a man, or woman, because he, or she, possessed them.

During the Second World War there was a shortage of sugar in Northern Ireland. It was rationed. Poteen makers substituted tins of syrup, which was more freely available, for packets of sugar in their brew. Pat remembers a man being taken to court because he was suspected of making poteen. His still was undiscovered but the 'law' had found a suspicious number of empty syrup tins on his premises. The man pleaded 'Not Guilty.' When asked to explain the large number of empty tins the man replied, 'Sir, it is not illegal to like syrup.' He was acquitted.

Fermentation is the first part of the poteen making process.

During fermentation the yeast becomes active and begins to grow. At first it feeds on the food (water, sugar, germinated barley, syrup, anything the poteen maker has put into his container), breathes in the oxygen dissolved in the water and gives out carbon dioxide.

(The carbon dioxide comes off as bubbles.) Yeast grows very rapidly using all the oxygen dissolved in its surroundings. At this point the fermentation process proper, begins. The yeast starts to break oxygen off the chemicals supplied by its food. It no longer gives off carbon dioxide. It gives off alcohol instead! Unfortunately for the yeast the alcohol builds up in the fermentating mixture. Yeast cannot live once the alcohol level reaches about 17%, so it is killed eventually and fermentation stops.

When fermentation ceases the poteen maker distils the brew by boiling it, making the alcohol evaporate so that it becomes stronger. The evaporated alcohol is led over a cold surface causing it to condense so that collection is possible.

Pat says 'poteen men' used to carry out their illicit trade in the bogs on top of the mountains. They hid containers, in which fermentation took place, in bog holes so that discovery was unlikely.

Fermentation outside occurred rapidly in warm weather but only slowly when the weather was inclement. Pat say he frequently met men, sneaking out furtively to their secret places in the bogs, with hot-water bottles hidden up their coats (to pack around the container in which fermentation was taking place), some extra sugar and a kettle of hot water to add to 'give the process a boost!'

Pat had a friend, who visited the site on the mountains, in which his poteen was brewing, on a cold winter night. A mist came down. The man became frightened. He could not see the way home and felt very lost. He was frightened of falling into a bog-hole, never to be seen again. He put the four fingers of each of his hands in his mouth and whistled for his black and white collie dog in the time honoured way of shepherds. He thought the dog would guide him home. Unfortunately the dog could not guide him home because there was no recognisable pad (track) through the bogs. So the man lay down and got the dog to lie on his feet. The heat from the dog's body on his feet prevented him from dying of exposure.

In the past, according to Pat, drunk men were guided along pads by their dogs, who took the responsibility of seeing their masters home. A pony or donkey could also bring its owner home, provided he held on to its tail!

Pat remembers meeting a tramp who always slept outside. Pat asked him how he managed to avoid suffering from exposure. The

The idea of sleeping under the stars horrifies me.

tramp told him that stones become heated by the sun during the day and that when he lay on the stones during the night heat was transferred into his body and he did not suffer from exposure, as long as he had a dog to cover his feet. In the past comparatively few people owned shoes so a dog would have been a comfort on cold bare feet.

Pat says he kept hearing rumours about how some women could make poteen in a kettle. He became very curious because he could not understand how it was done. According to Pat, a normal kettle spout would be very inefficient at allowing the alcohol to escape as it is too near the liquid.

Eventually Pat met a woman who said she made poteen in a kettle. Pat asked her how she did it and she explained that she had a large kettle especially made with the spout at the top instead of down the side. That gave sufficient space for the alcohol to come off efficiently. She collected the alcohol by having a bucket of cold water beside her. She placed plates in the bucket so that they became cold. She took one plate at a time out of the bucket, dried it and held it over the spout. The alcohol was collected in a basin which she held under the plate.

The woman said she felt her method of making poteen was ideal because she set the yeast and sugar to ferment in an innocent looking jar in a cupboard. It just looked as if she was making wine. The cupboard and the jar were clean and not likely to be contaminated in any way. The fermentation process took place rapidly because the jar was in the heat and that produced good poteen. Every household had a kettle so she could not be arrested because she possessed suspicious looking apparatus. Distillation, her way, was another innocent looking process. Who would bother looking twice at a woman working by the fire with a kettle and plates?

Pat says that a lot of the poteen produced in the past was very dangerous. Unscrupulous producers made brews that could be poisonous. They were worried about being caught so they threw anything they had around into their product - potato skins, beetroot, methylated spirits! (Sometimes 'good' poteen had beetroot which gave a pleasant taste and colour.) In this way a very alcoholic brew was produced in the minimum time possible. However, the alcohol came from the methylated spirits and corners were cut as far as hygiene was concerned. The resultant liquor could make people ill. The best poteen was obtained from people who just made a little for their own use and had a few bottles left over which they were prepared to give away or sell.

Ernest Scott remembers a neighbour making poteen then throwing the wash, that is residue left from making poteen, into a small pool on his farm. He had many ducks. The ducks drank water from the pool and became intoxicated. Ernest says nothing looks funnier than

I'm just a high flying, poteen-filled duck!

an inebriated duck staggering around a farmyard! The poteen residue did not have a lasting effect. The ducks recovered within a few hours.

Personally I believe the best Irish whiskey is produced legally and comes from Bushmills! Anyone who is interested in the production of Bushmills whiskey can visit the distillery, guided tours being available. Bushmills Distillery is the oldest licensed whiskey distillery in the world.

Chapter 6
FOOD, FERTILISER AND THINGS FROM SEAWEED

Cattle, sheep and horses found edible seaweed on the shore to eat during hard winters and late springs. Scientific testing has shown that the food value of knob wrack (Ascophyl lumnodosum), which grows about the middle of the shore, is almost equal to that of meadow hay. No wonder that small holders living beside the sea in County Down said that their sheep 'Kept fat and wholesome all winter and spring by feeding on the oare.'*

The following seaweeds were, and still are, eaten in Ireland:- Carrageen, or Irish Moss (Chrondus crispus), Sloke or Laver (Porphyra), Dulse (Rhodymenia), Dulaman (probably the channelled wrack, Pelvetia).

Seaweeds were taken as medicine, boiled and eaten with potatoes, or taken as what was known as 'kitchen', in other words a tasty morsel to be eaten between meals. During times when hunger stalked the land 'kitchen' might become the staple diet. J. Binns in his book 'Miseries and Beauties' described how in the 1830s hundreds of people could be seen going to the shore and collecting dulamen to eat.

Dulse is still fairly common, being sold in places such as Ballycastle, at the Auld Lammas Fair. In the past it was bought in spirit grocers and was always available in public houses, being given away because its salty taste made people thirsty

PREPARING SEAWEED TO EAT
It is very important to wash seaweed thoroughly if it is going to be eaten. It should either be used as soon as possible after being

*Oare is brown seaweed.

gathered, or it should be dried for consumption at a later date.
Seaweed should be dried by being laid on the grass exposed to the elements. If the weather is dry sprinkle with lots of fresh water. It will turn a creamy white colour after about a week. It must be exposed to the sunlight until thoroughly dried, then kept completely dry otherwise it will begin to rot.

CARRAGEEN MOSS

Carrageen Moss.

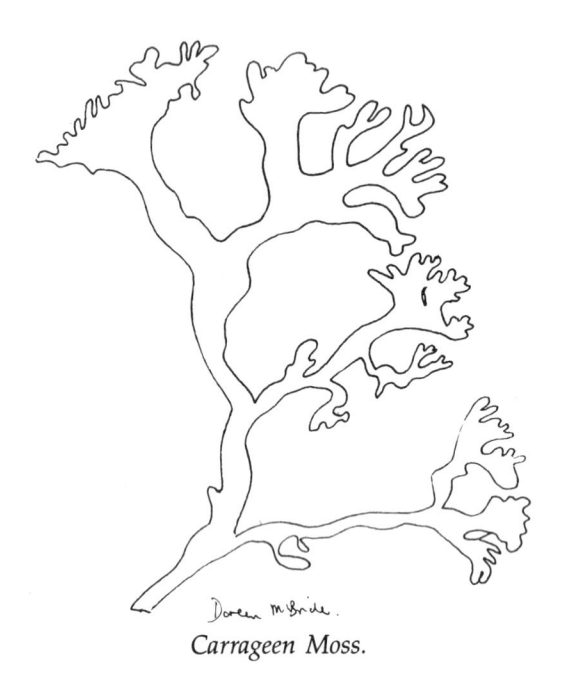

Carrageen moss is associated with Ireland to such an extent it is also known as Irish Moss although it is also common along the westerly Atlantic shores of Britain and Europe. It has many commercial uses including being sold as a health food and in the manufacture of jellies, ice-creams and soups.
Carrageen Moss has flat stalks with dark, purple-brown fronds which may be bleached to an off-white colour by the sun. It is a fan-shaped seaweed.

CARRAGEEN MOSS BLANCMANGE

6g (¼ oz) dried carrageen moss
½ litre (one pint) milk
6g (¼ oz) sugar
A little water

Steep the dried moss in the cold water for about 15 minutes.
Drain, trim off any 'root' or dark, discoloured parts.
Simmer in milk for about 30 minutes or until the mixture is thick enough to coat the back of a wooden spoon.
Stir in the sugar.
Serve hot.

The blancmange may be served with stewed fruit or it can be poured into a wetted mould and left to set.

Carrageen moss is an acquired taste so it may be advisable to add additional flavourings to the above recipe, such as chopped ginger, vanilla or grated lemon rind. Add to the mixture when it is simmering. People with a 'sweet tooth' will need more sugar.

CARRAGEEN JELLY

Carrageen jelly is made in the same way as carrageen blancmange with water substituted for milk.

DULSE

'At the auld Lammas Fair, boys, were ye ever there?
At the auld Lammas Fair in Ballycastle-oh?
Did you ever treat your Mary Anne to dulse and yella-man
At the auld Lammas Fair in Ballycastle-oh?'
                    (19th cent traditional song)

Dulse, which is found on the rocks at low tide, is a brownish red colour and grows to about 50 cm (18 ins) in size.

Dried dulse may be eaten as a savoury, or used as a relish, or added to a sauce or fish soup.

Dulse

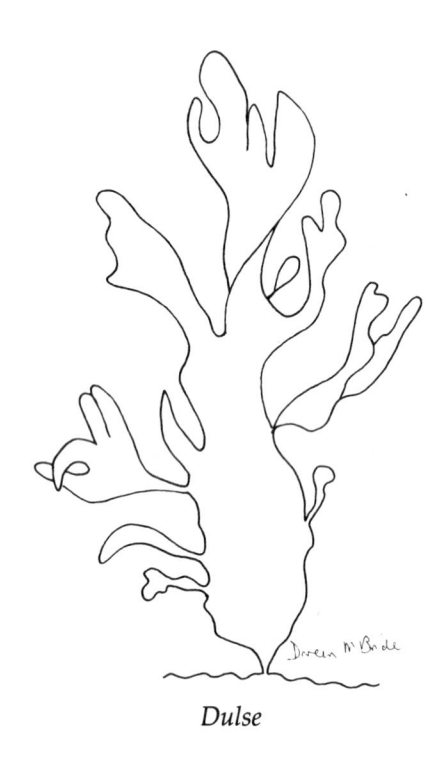

DULSE AS A VEGETABLE

Dried dulse
Water, milk or stock
Butter, salt and pepper
Soak dulse in water for at least 3 hours.
Simmer in milk or stock for an hour.
Strain.
Re-heat.
Add a good-sized lump of butter and seasonings.
The flavour of dulse in enhanced if it is served with a good white sauce.

Seaweeds were used not only to feed animals and people, they were also used, and indeed still are used, to feed the land in the form of fertilisers. Ernest Scott recalls that seaweeds are most beneficial when used inland, away from the influence of the sea, and that they kept corn crops from 'lodging', that is being beaten flat by the rain.

Fertilisers are vital for good crop yields. Smallholders who lived near the sea often made use of the seaweeds. The custom persists in parts of Ireland to the present day. I saw seaweed covering the ground between plants in a beautiful garden beside the sea near Ballyvaughan, County Clare in December 1990.

In the past all types of seaweeds were used as fertilisers, the oar weeds which are found at very low tide, extending into the ocean, the bladder wracks that cover the middle shore and the channelled wrack found on the upper shore. In Ballyvaughan the ground was covered with bladder wracks.

Seaweed is a valuable fertiliser because it contains roughly the same amount of nitrogen as farm-yard manure and about twice the amount of potassium, as well as organic matter. Sandy soils have a tendency to be deficient in potassium because water drains through quickly and potassium is washed away. Seaweed is particularly good for them. Its gelatinous nature improves their ability to hold water.

Oarweeds and wracks are especially good for growing potatoes although the salt content may make the tubers waxy. Farmers avoided this by ploughing the seaweed into the ground in the late autumn, or by making it into a compost.

As a general rule, seaweeds are deficient in lime and phosphates, having about one third of the phosphorus content of farmyard manure.

Seaweed had to be spread on the land every year because the effects do not last as long as those obtained from farm-yard manure. The salt in seaweed was thought to act as a condiment because cattle and sheep love to eat the grass on which it has been used. They were thought to thrive better and grow faster than on ground fertilised with manure. Ernest Scott, who farmed in Ballynure, County Antrim, remembers obtaining a 'salt lick' for animals living inland, on land which did not have the benefit of seaweed. The salt lick was a block of rock salt, which he got from the salt mines at Carrickfergus, and placed in a field along with his cattle. The cattle went and licked the salt.

There are different theories about how seaweed should be used. In some places people believed that it should be spread directly over the ground, which was the method I saw in County Clare at Ballyvaughan. In other parts of the country it was believed to be best to compost the seaweed before using it. Sometimes seaweed

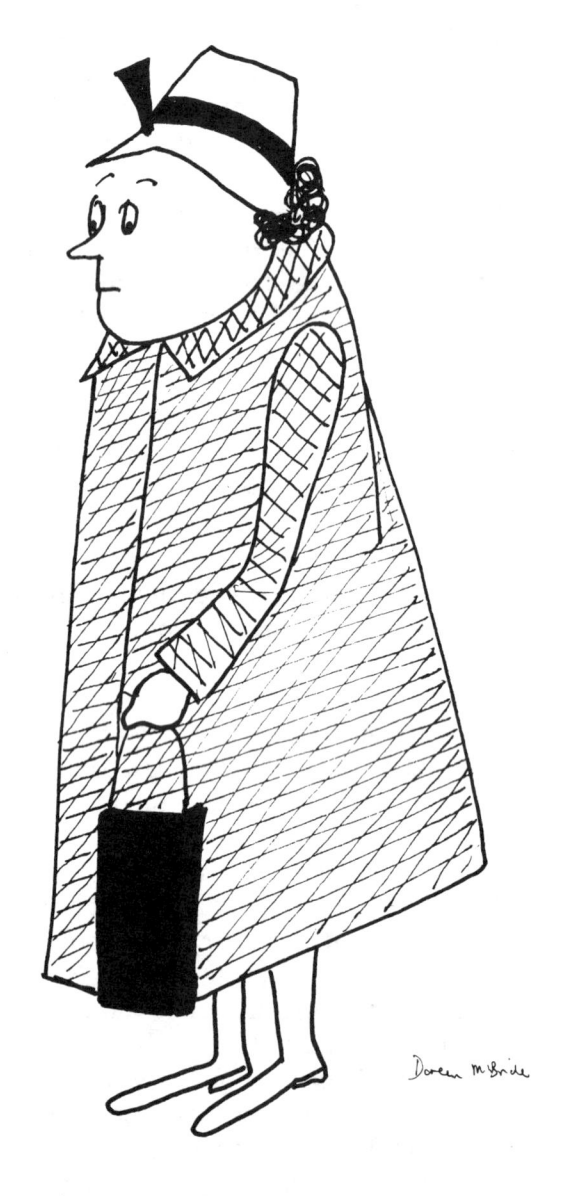

See me? See my man? See dulse? Can't stand it!

compost heaps were covered with soil, occasionally the seaweed was added in layers to manure heaps and occasionally it was mixed with peat moss as this helped fermentation to take place more quickly.

Tom Porter, a local poet and historian who lives in Newcastle, at the foot of the Mourne Mountains in County Down, told me that in Mourne Country bladder wrack (Fucus vesiculosis) was known locally as 'box' while serrated wrack (Fucus serratus) was called 'cam tails', and that in the Mourne Country the wrack was 'skailed' (spread) on the land. It was placed directly into drills for potatoes and turnips. 'Cam tails' had the reputation for being particularly good for growing turnips and marigolds.

Box seaweed was used to cure smelly feet. It was boiled in water for 30 minutes, the liquid cooled and used to bathe the feet as required.

All the access roads to the shore along the Mourne coast were originally wrack-roads. One or two are still named as such although the interpretation of the local council of the local dialect has led to spelling mistakes, such as 'Wreck Road'!

One of the wrack roads, which is to be found one mile north of Annalong, had a gate which was controlled by the local farmers.

Yum! Yum! Mummy — seaweed fertiliser!

INBLOWN WRACK

The wind's been blowing hard all night,
There's white water in the bay;
There's big black clouds out to the east,
There'll be wrack at the shore the day.

Get up and get out to the stable,
And harness the black mare,
And get to the Springwell loanin'
Before half the townland's there.

And take a look for cam tails,
They're better than the box,
And mind you don't cowp the cart,
Among the slippy rocks.

Take a load to the Whinny Beatins,
And a load to the Rocky Hill,
And maybe you should take one
To the jib behind the mill.

And don't get into trouble,
Take no more than your share,
Unless of course you're early
And there's none of the others there.

But if the crowd has gathered,
And you have to wait your turn,
Take a load to the Tammocks,
From the gut at the Lady's Burn.

S. T. Porter (Mourne Ballads)

The gate was locked one day a year to retain the right of way. The gate post still exists.

In some areas such as Strangford Lough and Carlingford Lough, County Down, stones were placed on the shore to grow wrack. Mill Bay, Carlingford Lough, on the edge of Mourne Country, is particularly interesting. The wrack beds are half-acre rectangles set with rows of boulders of about 30cm (one foot) in diameter. These wrack beds are still visible at low tide. Many of the beds are subdivided into smaller 'cuts' so that they could be sub-let. Access was by narrow lanes between the beds. Around Mill Bay as many as a hundred carts could converge at low tide. Sometimes fights broke out as cart-owners disputed rights of access! Some farmers used creels, designed for carrying wrack, on donkeys. Many creels had a 'quick release bottom' to facilitate emptying.

There were established traditions, which varied from district to district, relating to the distribution of seaweeds.

Until recent times one of the most profitable ways of using seaweed was in the manufacture of kelp. Kelp was made by burning the thick stems of sea-tangle (Laminaria) and/or other coarse weeds

Kelp beds, Carlingford Lough.

which are thrown up by winter storms or which may be cut at low tide. The name 'kelp' may mean either the weed or the ash of the weed.

The weeds were dried on low stone walls. They rot easily in rain so they had to be turned repeatedly in wet weather. Once dried, they were built up into a structure called a rick. A thatch was placed

Wall used to burn kelp, Co. Antrim.

on top of the rick to keep the contents dry. The kelp was placed in a kiln on the shore during fine days in summer. Each kiln burnt for many hours and consumed many tons of seaweed. The weed was fed into the fire a little at a time. It was said that 60 tons of weed were needed to produce 1 ton of kelp. If the supply of driftweed was not sufficient for the farmers' needs the heavy tangles, growing below the low tide mark, were cut with knives mounted on handles, which could be up to twenty feet long, so that the best weeds, free of sand, growing in comparatively deep water, could be reached. The smell of the dense, oily smoke from kelp burning drifted far inland.

Men wielded their long knives, cutting the wrack as they sat in boats made from skins stretched over a wooden frame. Women dragged the weed ashore. Cutting wrack was hard, filthy work. In some places, such as the Rosses in County Donegal, rents were paid in kelp. Surplus kelp was bartered for spirits and tobacco, which both men and women enjoyed.

Kelp was used to make soap, bleaching materials and glass.

Sometimes very wet weather made it impossible to collect sufficent turf as fuel. Seaweed was burnt instead, as suggested by the traditional rhyme:-

'Ameracam the stinking hole,
Burn the wrack and save the coal.'

Ameracam is a district near Soldier's Point in the Mourne Country.

Old Wrack Road, Mourne country, 1990.

Chapter 7
POTATOES

In Ireland potatoes are commonly called 'spuds', 'murphys' and sometimes 'spud murphys'. Potatoes, with the addition of milk or buttermilk, form a scientifically balanced diet. According to the oral tradition potatoes formed the staple diet of people in poorer areas, so they were the most important crop.

Potatoes were boiled, then placed in a basket made of unpeeled willow rods and allowed to drain. If fish was served it was put on top of the potatoes and eaten with the fingers. The most usual way to eat the potatoes was to place salt and water or milk in a saucer and dip the potatoes into it.

Potatoes left over from the meal were saved. They might be pushed into the embers of the fire for any hungry person who called to eat, or they could be turned into potato-cake or fadge. They were also used to make rousel, which was a mixture of potatoes, oatmeal and buttermilk, made into a dough and formed into a large, flat, rounded shape approximately 5 cms (2 inches) in depth. Rousel was baked on a griddle like soda bread. School children took cold potatoes to school for lunch. Sometimes they gave their largest potatoes to their schoolmaster.

Fishermen carried potatoes with them on their voyages. Potatoes were also used to feed livestock. In other words, potatoes provided a plentiful supply of cheap food which was easily grown. The standard of living at the time was such that a diet of nothing but potatoes was not thought to be a hardship. Poor people who did not have enough to eat undercooked their potatoes because hard, undercooked potatoes are more difficult to digest than soft ones. They stay in the stomach for a longer time and cut down the number of hunger pains felt.

Meat was rarely eaten except at Easter or Christmas. Many families could not afford to eat meat and even those who reared a pig were forced to sell it to pay the rent.

Famines were caused by failure of potato crops.

Potato crop failed because of potato blight fungus, Phytophthora infestans. Spores of the fungus landed on the potato leaves, grew down through a leaf pore and rapidly killed the plant. If rain washed the fungus off the leaves it entered the ground and attacked potato tubers, turning them rotten and stinking.

A chemical spray, Bordeaux Mixture, was developed in France during the 1880s. It was found to control potato blight. Copper sulphate, which had been used to prevent fungus from growing on vines, was the main ingredient.

Potatoes have to be buried 10-15 cm (2-3 inches) deep. Most ploughs work well only on large areas of flat ground so farmers with only a couple of acres of land and those with small, hilly, rocky fields used a spade to plant potatoes.

Ireland has many different types of soil and the soil, like the scenery, varies remarkably over an extremely small area. The rich, deep soil at the top of a drumlin may be entirely different from the wet soil near the bottom and different from that found in the bog between drumlins.

The wide variation in soil led to the evolution of many different types of spade. In the 1850s a spade mill would have manufactured over 200 types of spade. As a result farmers living next door to each other could have used entirely different types of spade to plant their potatoes.

Potatoes were planted in 'lazy beds'. The first step in making a 'lazy bed' was to spread fertiliser in strips along the ground. Seed potatoes were placed in rows along the fertiliser strips. Sods of grass were then turned up to cover the potatoes and loose earth, dug from the furrows, was spread on top. Many signs of lazy beds, abandoned because of depopulation, may be seen around the countryside either under the heather on hilltops or in grass covered ridges that streak across fields. They are most easily seen when the sun is low in the sky or in frosty or snowy weather.

Lazy beds had several advantages. The grass which was turned under formed humus. The fertiliser was spread where it was of most benefit. It was necessary to dig only half the ground, so lazy beds were labour saving, and the furrows formed gave good drainage which is essential for growing potatoes in Ireland's wet climate.

Lazy beds were also formed with the help of swing ploughs.

Fertiliser was spread in long strips along the field and the seed potatoes were set on top of it. Drill ploughs were used to push earth over the potatoes.

Ernest Scott remembers ploughing potato fields using 'half Clydesdales' horses. Clydesdales are huge. They tower over most other horse breeds and are only suitable for work on large farms. A 'half Clydesdale' was the offspring of a Clydesdale stallion and an Irish mare. Clydesdales are strong and placid while Irish mares had a lot of spirit. According to Ernest, their offspring inherited the best characteristics of both breeds. Such a horse would never 'rust', that is refuse to work! Larger than a normal horse but smaller than a full bred animal, these big horses were trained to walk with the elegance of mannequins. They were led repeatedly up and down a furrow beside unploughed ground. It is very uncomfortable walking with one foot up and one foot down, so the horse learned to place its feet accurately in a straight line. Training made this mincing manner of walking second nature.

It was very important for horses working in potato fields to place their feet accurately in a straight line because a hoof out of place led to crop damage. Farmers wanting to buy horses had the animal led up and down in front of them so it was possible to watch footwork and other points of interest.

There is a story around Ballynure district about the local photographer, W. A. Green, whose work forms The Green

Mourne country. Traces of lazy beds may still be seen in country such as this, March 1991.

I may be big, but I'm a lovely mover.

Collection held in the Ulster Folk and Transport Museum, Cultra, County Down. Apparently Green became fascinated by horses. He visited the Ballyclare Fair, set up his camera and disappeared under the covering of black velvet necessary in those days. He asked a farmer to run his horse towards the camera so he could photograph it.

The farmer very obligingly ran the horse towards Green several times, turning the animal beside the photographer. As the animal turned beside Green its bowels moved and its droppings fell over his trousers and feet. As Green came out from under his coverings he noticed the state of his feet and legs and swore profusely. The farmer turned back towards Green and said 'I owe you an apology for that!'

Green looked at him 'Do you?' he smiled, his temper abated, 'I thought it was the horse!'

Martha Kerr was born in 17 Bloomfield Street, Belfast. She remembered that her father, Enoch Kerr, had what was known as 'a plot' in the Beersbridge area, which he used to produce vegetables, including potatoes, for his family. 'Plots' were very common in Belfast until the 1950s after which they gradually fell into disuse.

A piece of land was sub-divided into small 'plots' which were then cultivated by different families.

Enoch tended his plot carefully making sure the soil was in good condition. He was most insistent that his potatoes were planted on Saint Patrick's Day because he believed that without the luck brought by the Saint, his potatoes would not thrive. He had a thick stick with a pointed end which he used to 'dibble' a hole in the ground. Martha came behind him, carrying seed potatoes in her apron and dropped one into each hole and covered it up.

In mild parts of the country, such as County Kerry, potatoes were often left in the ground through the winter. In other parts of the country they were lifted with spades or forks.

'Tattie howking', as it was called, was dirty tiring work. Basically men dug the potatoes out of the ground. They were followed by women crawling on their hands and knees, lifting the potatoes uncovered by the men and placing them into two baskets which they dragged behind them. Young men carried the full baskets and emptied their contents into barrels left in the field for that purpose. Wet weather made the potato harvest one of the most unpleasant tasks of the year. It was difficult for the men to dig in driving rain and absolutely killing for the women as they crawled through mud on their hands and knees, dragging heavy, clay encrusted baskets behind them.

Ploughs were also used to harvest potatoes, grown in drills. Men used spades to clear the potato stalks. The plough was set so that it penetrated the soil below the level at which the deepest potato would be found. It then cut along one side of the bed. The labourers followed the plough and collected the potatoes.

In the past potatoes were usually stored in 'clamps', also called 'bings'. A potato clamp could be any length. It was between 1 and 2 metres (3-6 feet) in width and was simply a place where potatoes were piled along an imaginary straight line in a gently rounded heap. The heap of potatoes was covered with straw, rushes or sedge grass. The clamp was completed by being covered with earth which was beaten firm by the back of a shovel.

The clamp was opened when potatoes were needed, the tubers removed and the clamp resealed. Potatoes taken out of clamps at the end of winter were much fresher than those stored inside buildings.

Chapter 8
THE MAGIC OF DYE PLANTS

Ernest Scott remembers how important natural dyes were during his youth. Each factory associated with making cloth had an expert who was responsible for dyeing. The expert scoured the countryside looking for plants which could be used to produce natural dyes.

Some dye plants were imported. Logwood is a dye plant imported from the Southern States of America. Importation of logwood began during the slave trade. Slave ships went out from Europe filled with bodies. It was uneconomic and dangerous to sail empty ships back to Europe. They had no ballast so timber was loaded into the boats, taken to Europe and sold. Logwood was one of the timbers imported. The logwood was processed in mills. Ireland has many roads which where named after the logwood mills, some of which, such as that near Ballynure in County Antrim, still exist today long after their namesakes have disappeared.

Dye plants are peculiar things because the plant colour gives no clue to the colour of the dye obtained from it. The green leaves of willow produce a yellow dye, brown onion skins a yellow gold dye and purple foxglove flowers give a pale green dye!

Many dye plants give a faint aromatic smell to the material on which they have been used. The characteristic smell of Donegal tweed comes from the dye plants used.

There are coloured substances inside plants called pigments. To produce a natural dye, simply boil the plant in water. The pigments will come out of the plant into the water to give a dye colour. Unfortunately this dye is not 'fast'. It will wash out of the material on which it has been used, so something is needed to make the dye stick. In other words, a 'mordant' must be used. Tin, alum, iron and chrome are good mordants. They act like magic because they can change the colour of the dye. Meadow-sweet roots give a rosy-red colour when alum is used as a mordant, chocolate brown when chrome is the mordant and grey-black when iron is the mordant. The explanation is very simple. The pigments which form the dyes are easily changed. A change not only alters their chemical composition but also their colour. If a white flower such as a daisy, snowdrop, lily or apple blossom is held over a bottle of concentrated ammonium it will turn yellow. The fumes from the ammonium alter the chemical composition inside the flower making a pigment found in yellow flowers. So the white flower turns yellow!

Pigments may change when growing inside plants. Flowers may differ in colour because of the temperature, type of soil and so on. Just think of the hydrangea so commonly grown in Irish gardens. Blue flowered hydrangea transported from an acid to an alkaline soil will begin to produce pink flowers. Similarly if an acid soil is limed the flowers will turn pink because lime counteracts the soil's acidity. It is also known that a handful of rusty nails tossed on top of the soil where a hydrangea is growing will change its colour.

Some of the dye recipes from the past sound absolutely revolting. A purple dye called Cudbear was made from lichens (Ochrelechia tartarea and Ureolaria calcarea). The lichens were ground up and mixed with males' urine. Males' urine was thought to be stronger

"Man dear! It's like magic."

than that of female! The urine was collected in a big pot, probably set behind the house. Young men were frequently reminded not to 'waste piddle on the hedge, but to put it in the pot!'

The dye from plants varies according to the time of the year, some dyes being stronger in autumn, others in spring. The soil type will also alter the colour. The usual amount of dyestuffs to use is 500 gm (1 lb.) of roots, bark, berries, leaves or flowers to 500 gms (1 lb.) wool. It is important to use natural wools rather than white, which has probably been treated to help prevent staining, so it will not pick dyes up easily. Natural Aran type wool bought from shops is very suitable for experimenting. Synthetic fibres do not give satisfactory results with natural dyes.

In the past people spun wool from a sheep's fleece. It is still possible to buy a sheep's fleece from a farmer at shearing time and some people with sufficient space still keep a sheep to provide a fleece for spinning. (Sheep can make surprisingly affectionate pets.)

Once the wool has been obtained, the first step is to use a mordant so that the dye is fast and will not disappear at the first wash. Today mordants may be bought at chemist shops. Here is a list of common mordants with their scientific names and the amount needed for 500gm (1 lb) of wool.

Mordant	Scientific name	Amount
Alum	Potassium Aluminium Sulphate	(3 ozs)
Ammonia	Ammonium Hydroxide Solution (urine was used in the past instead of ammonium hydroxide)	1 part to 2 parts water
Copper	Copper Sulphate	(½ oz)
Iron	Ferrous sulphate	(½ oz)
Salt	Sodium chloride (table salt)	(3 ozs)
Tannin	Tannic Acid (oak or alder twigs were used in the past)	(3 ozs)
Tin	Stannous Chloride	(½ oz)

Some mordants are poisonous so they should be kept away from children. It is advisable to wear rubber gloves when mordanting and dyeing. Sufficient water should be added to cover the wool and

LIST OF PLANTS WHICH MAY BE USED FOR NATURAL DYEING

Plant	Part of plant used	Mordant	Colour
Bracken	Buds	Alum	lime-green
	young shoots	Alum	creamy yellow
	young shoots	Iron	dull green
Beetroot	Cooked skin, roots juice	unmordanted	magenta
Blackberries	berries	Alum	blue-grey
	berries	Tin	blue
	young shoots	Iron	dark grey
	young shoots	Alum	fawn
Coffee		Alum	coffee
Crab apple	fruit	Alum	pink
Dandelion	flowerheads	Tin	yellow
Elderberry	leaves	Alum	pale yellow
	berries	Alum	lavender
Nettle	flowers	Alum	dull gold
	leaves	Alum	green-yellow
Onion	skins	Alum	yellow-gold
	skins	Iron	moss green
	skins	Tin	tan-orange
Privet	leaves	Alum	yellow
	ripe berries	Alum	grey-green
Purple cabbage	leaves	Alum	lavender-blue
Ragwort	flowerheads	Alum	yellow
Tea		Alum	tan
Whins	flowerheads	Salt	yellow
	flowerheads	Alum	yellow

allow it to move around freely.

Mordants should be properly dissolved before adding wool, otherwise dyeing will be uneven.

Generally speaking, mordants and wool should be boiled together for about 40 minutes.

Mordanted wool may be dyed immediately, or dried and stored to be dyed at a later date, by boiling with a dye plant. The longer wool is left to boil with a dye plant the stronger the colour. Thirty minutes is usually sufficient.

Dyeing may be done in a washing machine although it will need to be washed out afterwards if the next wash is not to be tinted as well. In the past dyeing was done in large galvanised iron pots over the fire. Separate pots were kept for cooking and for dyeing.

In the past people had very few clothes. Many people spent their lives in clothes which were ragged to such a degee that they were immodest. If 'good clothes' were owned they were looked after carefully. Clothes made from black, or navy-blue cloth, kept for social or solemn occasions such as funerals, sometimes for most of a lifetime, became shiny at the elbows and seats after years of use. They were revitalised by being sponged with liquid produced by boiling 50 ivy leaves in 500cc (1 pint) of water. In the past redyeing faded clothes was a busy urban industry.

Chapter 9
PLANTS USED TO CURE DISEASE

The medicines we use today did not exist in the past. There was no National Health Service and the majority of people were so poor that they could not afford to go to a doctor. Doctors were called as a last resort. Most people used simple remedies made from common plants found locally, such as whins discussed in an earlier chapter, in an attempt to cure disease.

The advent of modern medicine caused the simple tried and tested cures of the past to fall into disuse. Country cures are not as quick-acting, or as strong, as the chemicals we have today. However, they have fewer side effects and many of the cures of the past should find a place alongside our modern drugs.

The list of plants below used as country cures is a long way from being comprehensive. It is simply a series of very common, easy to identify, plants.

Many of the old cure plants are delicious to eat and some, such as nettles, are becoming fashionable in upmarket restaurants in Ireland so a few recipes have been provided.

I personally have had a lot of pleasure and fun using recipes from the past, cooking things commonly called 'weeds' and serving them to visitors. There is an old saying 'What the eye does not see the stomach does not grieve over!'

If I am ill I go to a medical doctor, but I feel there is no harm in experimenting with 'weeds' provided I enjoy the taste. If they have a reputation as preventive medicine or as a cure so much the better! However, it is advisable to make sure that plants are identified properly because many are poisonous. Plants should not be collected from places which have been sprayed with weedkillers or insecticides and they should not be dug up, unless they are on your own land.

BLACKBERRIES

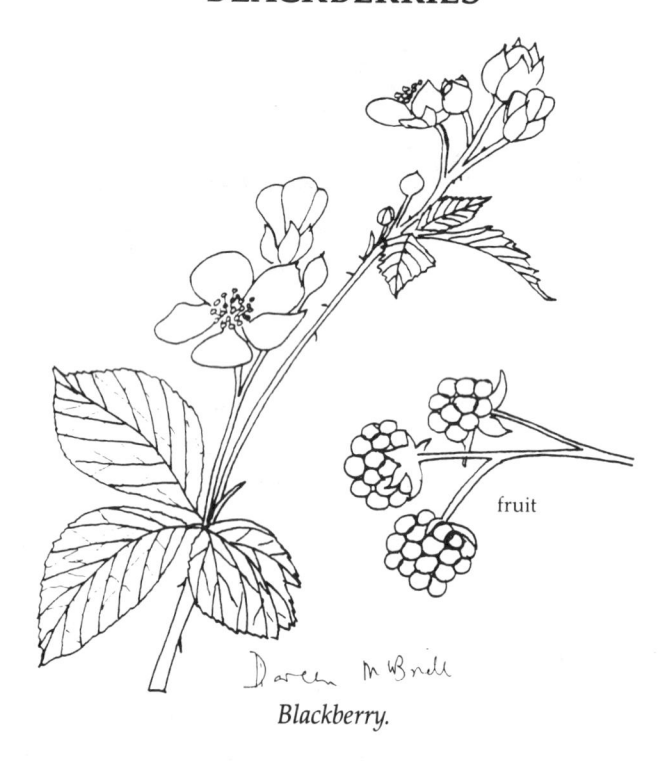

Blackberry.

Blackberries are very common in hedgerows, scrublands and woods. Their stems may be as long as 5 metres (15 feet) and the flowers vary in colour from white to cerise. The flowering period is from May to September.

Blackberry briars are very pliable so they were used in basket making as they could easily be bent round upright canes.

Blackberries may be picked, washed and eaten raw, stewed, used as a filling for a pie, made into jam, syrup or wine. The fruits contain Vitamin C.

Nora Bates grew up in Saintfield, County Down. She came from a large family who knew poverty. Nora remembers collecting blackberries during the summer months and earning a little money by selling them for jam making. She used to set off early in the day with her sisters. They carried buckets and baskets to place the fruit in, took a few sandwiches for lunch and spent the whole day collecting the wild fruits. Then they carried their heavy buckets and baskets back to the village and sold their wares to the village women. They came back exhausted, but happy, although their hands, arms and legs were scratched by thorns.

Norah's father used to collect blackberries in large barrels, load the barrels on to his cart and take them to Millar's Jam Making Factory in Belfast, where he earned a little extra money by selling them. Norah was very upset when her father sold his horse and cart in the late 1940s and replaced them by a second-hand hearse bought from Minnis, the local undertaker. She hated seeing her father load blackberries into the hearse and disliked the idea of being a passenger. Her father found the hearse more convenient than his horse and cart and he used it for all sorts of commercial jobs, such as transporting furniture.

Pat Cassidy remembers an unusual use being made of a stout, thick briar cut from a blackberry patch. Pat went to school during the 1920s. There was a boy in his class who hated school. This boy lived with a granny, who was confined to bed and an aunt, who was so stiff that she could not bend down. One day he decided not to go to school and got under his bed thinking that he could not be reached. The aunt took the stout blackberry cane, lay on the

Norah's father, niece and family horse.

bed and used it to 'wallop' up and down under the bed. The boy came out screaming in pain, covered in scratches where the blackberry thorns had hit him. He always appeared willing to go to school after that!

BLACKBERRY FOOL

225g (½ lb) blackberries
Few drops vanilla essence
Sugar to taste
Whipping cream
Place fruit in pot
Cover fruit with water
Cook slowly until berries are soft
Add few drops vanilla essence
Add sugar to taste
Stir until sugar is melted
Either put through a sieve or put in a liquidiser
Allow to cool
Whip cream and fold into blackberries
Place in fridge before serving

BLACKBERRY AND APPLE SWEET

4-6 apples
500g (1 lb) blackberries
Sugar or honey
Cream flavoured with a little whiskey, if liked
Mash blackberries to a pulp
Sweeten with sugar or honey
Wash and core apples
Stuff apples with blackberry mixture
Place in fireproof dish and bake in moderate oven for 30 minutes
Serve with cream

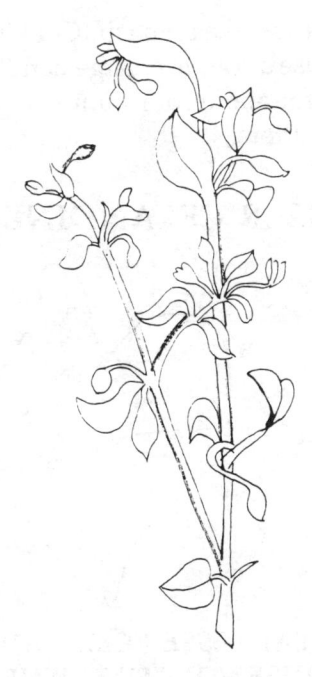

CHICKWEED

Chickweed.

Chickweed, which was once very common, is a pale green, sprawling plant which spreads over soils that have not been deeply cultivated. It is not nearly as common on farm land as in days gone by because modern methods of cultivation turn the soil over much more deeply than those used in the past. Chickweed seeds cannot begin to grow if they are buried deeply in soil.

Chickweed shoots and leaves are pale green. The flowers, which are small and white appear throughout the year but mainly in spring and summer.

If the juice from chickweed is squeezed on boils it will help them to heal. The plant is full of Vitamin C so it helps to prevent colds. In the past it was also used to prevent scurvy.

Chickweed may be eaten raw or it may be cooked. To eat raw use as a salad, simply collect young, whole plants. Wash them carefully and either serve whole or chop them up. They taste nice mixed with a salad dressing made from lemon juice and salad oil. They also taste good when mixed with other vegetables or in a sandwich along with marmite.

Cooked chickweed tastes like spinach. Cooking reduces its bulk by about two-thirds so use a couple of large handfuls for each person and boil in salty water for about four minutes. Serve with salt and pepper or with herb butters.

LESSER CELANDINE

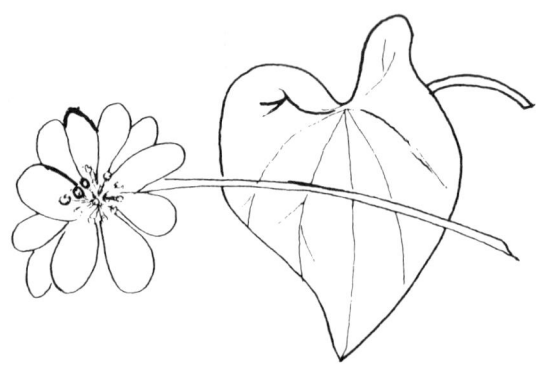

WARNING: DO NOT EAT LESSER CELANDINES. THEY ARE POISONOUS AND CAUSE VOMITING WHEN SWALLOWED.

The bright yellow flowers of Lesser Celandines look very like those of a buttercup. Close examination shows that buttercup petals are rounded while those of the Lesser Celandine are pointed. Buttercup leaves are matt and hairy, Lesser Celandine leaves are shiny and a brighter green colour than those of buttercups.

Lesser Celandines grow to a height of 20 cms, they bloom from March to May and their stems are a brownish colour. They are very common in damp places.

Both Lesser Celandines and buttercups are poisonous. They must not be eaten.

In the past Lesser Celandines were used to cure piles, a common name for the plant being pilewort. The roots of the Lesser Celandine are white and bulbous. People used to dig them up, pound them with a little urine, or wine, and apply them to piles where they reduced swelling.

CLOVER

Clover.

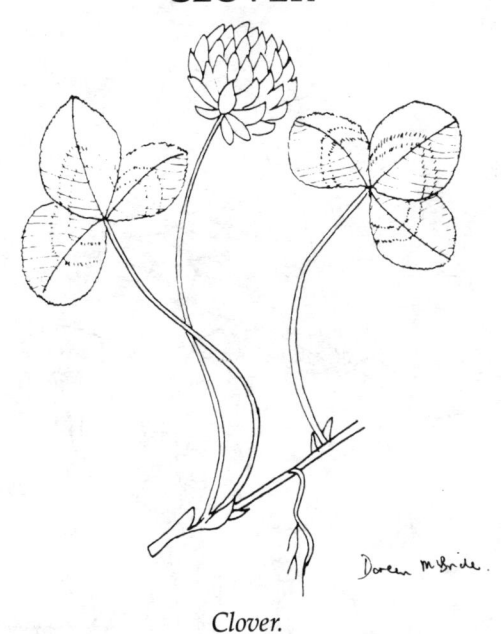

Clover grows in grassy places. It is a sprawling plant with a height of about 30 cm. There are two types of clover, red clover and white clover. The flowering period is from May to September. White clover imported from New Zealand was ploughed into the ground to act as a fertiliser.

Legend tells that St. Patrick once bent down to the ground and picked up a leaf. This leaf was divided into three sections. St. Patrick used it to describe the Trinity, the three in one, Father, Son and Holy Ghost. Scientists do not know which plant St. Patrick used. It was called 'shamrock' but no-one knows what the 'shamrock' was. There are four possibilities, wood sorrel, hop-trefoil, bird's foot trefoil and clover.

Sometimes it is possible to find a four-leafed clover. This is thought to be very, very lucky. Clover makes an excellent fodder crop for cattle, hence the expression 'living in clover'.

Young clover leaves are edible. They may be added to salads, soups and stews or cooked and eaten like spinach. Fresh clover flowerheads make a pleasant substitute for tea. Clover tea helps cure chest colds, diarrhoea and stomach upsets.

COLT'S FOOT

Colt's Foot.

Colt's foot has yellow flowers, which appear during the months of January and February, before the leaves develop. On first sight colt's foot flowers look similar to those of the dandelion, however, the flower stems are entirely different. Colt's foot stems appear solid and scaly while dandelion stems are smooth, shiny and hollow. The leaves give colt's foot its name. They are said to have the same shape as a colt's foot imprint. When the leaves first appear they are small. They grow steadily throughout the season until they become large and very conspicuous. The young colt's foot flowerheads are collected before they open and used medically, mainly in herbal teas to treat coughs, catarrh, asthma, bronchitis and laryngitis. Fresh, washed, crushed, Colt's Foot leaves may be applied to skin inflammations and rheumatic joints to cure them.

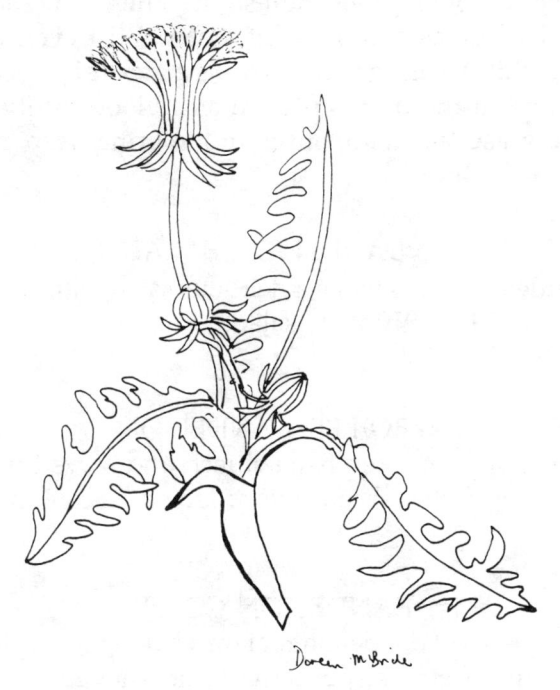

DANDELION

Dandelion.

Dandelions have unbranched, hollow stems and bright yellow flowers. The main flowering period is from May to September, but it is possible to find Dandelions in flower during mid-winter in mild spells. They are very common and grow to a height of 35 cm (15 ins).

When I was a child growing up in Belfast I was frightened to touch dandelions because I was told by the other children who lived in the same street that they were called 'pee-the-beds'. I did not want to suffer the humiliation of wetting the bed! There is a certain amount of justification for the old name 'pee-the-bed' because dandelions do have a diuretic effect on the kidneys making them pass more urine than usual. This effect helps to wash infections and stones out from the kidneys and their urinary tracts. In the past people either made tea from dandelion leaves to increase the output of urine, or they boiled the whole plant, roots and all, then drank the liquid.

In folk lore the effect of dandelions on the kidneys has been exaggerated out of all proportion so that there is tendency to fight shy of it. I know as a child I felt worried if I even walked on a dandelion while wearing shoes! This is a great pity because it tastes delicious and in the past was used as a blood purifier, a remedy for heart disease, as an appetiser and to bring deep, restful sleep.

DANDELION SALAD

Young dandelion leaves make a delicious salad, either eaten on their own, or mixed in with other salads.

BOILED DANDELION

The leaves may be cooked like spinach and served plain, or with herb butter, or garlic, sliced onion, lemon juice and spices.

DANDELION COFFEE

Place small pieces of dandelion root on a baking tray in a moderately slow oven. Turn frequently and roast until they turn a rusty brown colour. Roasted roots may be ground and made into coffee.

DANDELION SYRUP

150g (6 oz) dandelion flowers
150g (6 oz) sugar
350ccs (²⁄₃ pint) water
Pour boiling water on top of dandelion flowers
Leave standing for 24 hours
Strain
Add sugar
Boil until the solution reaches the consistency of syrup
Bottle
Sterilise by placing lidded bottles in a saucepan of water so that they do not touch the bottom or each other in case they break. Bring to boil and simmer for 30 minutes.

DOG ROSE

Dog Rose.

Dog Roses are found in scrub, woods and hedgerows. They grow to a height of 3m (9 feet) and have flowers, which vary in colour from white to a deep pink and appear during June and July. The bright red fruits appear in autumn

Any rose with a good perfume may be eaten. Deep red roses are usually the most fragrant and so are nicest to eat. Pull the petals from the flower, wash them and throw the tasteless base away. Mix with fruit or vegetable salad. Rose petals may also be covered with chocolate and used as cake decorations.

Rose hips are full of Vitamin C. Rosehip Syrup is made very simply. It was once given by the Health Service in Northern Ireland to mothers for their babies and small children. It is full of Vitamin C and tastes very sweet so that most babies and small children love it.

ROSE HIP SYRUP

1 kg (2 lb) rosehips
500g (1 lb) sugar
1½ litres water (3 pints)

Remove the seeds found inside the hips. (This is very important because the seeds are covered in irritating hairs which are especially damaging to children. The seeds are easily removed, as anyone who has opened a rose hip and used the seeds as itching powder to push down a friend's back, will know!)

Mince, grate or crush the fruit.
Place fruit into ¾ litre (1½ pints) boiling water.
Bring back to boiling point.
Remove from heat.
Allow to stand for 15 minutes.
Strain through a jelly bag.

Return juice to cooking pot which has been thoroughly cleaned of all pulp etc.

Add ¾ litres (1½ pints) boiling water.
Boil juice together until reduced by one half.
Warm 500 gm (1 lb) sugar.
Add warmed sugar to juice.
Stir sugar until it dissolves.
Boil for another 5 minutes.
Pour into warmed bottles while still hot.
Seal immediately.

Sterilise by arranging the bottles in a saucepan of water so that they do not touch either the bottom or the sides of the saucepan, or each other.
Simmer for 30 minutes.

ROSE HIP TEA

Ripe hips of the dog rose were infused to make tea which was drunk as a cure for colds.

ELDER

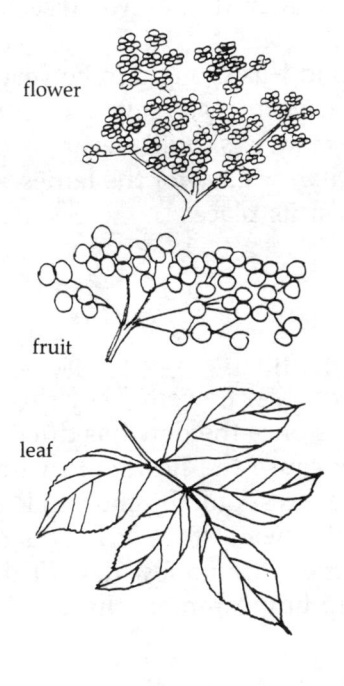

Elder.

The elder grows into a small tree of about 7m (21 ft) in height. It has creamy-white flowers during the months of May and June. These are followed by fruits which are black whenever they are ripe. An elder tree bearing ripe and unripe fruits appears marvellous in the sun after a shower of rain. The unripe fruits are green, they turn red and finally go black. After rain the tree can look as if it is covered with green, red and black jewels, glistening in the sunshine.

There is a lot of folk lore associated with the elder. In the past all the herbs were thought to be under the protection of the elder which was regarded as the Queen of the forest. It was thought necessary to ask the Queen Mother's permission, before picking or cutting her wood, by saying:- 'Lady Elder, give me some of thy wood and then will I also give thee some of mine when it grows in the forest'.

People believed that permission would be readily granted but if it was not sought the Elder Mother would seek revenge by bringing bad luck.

Burning elder wood was thought to be very unlucky. The smell of the elder smoke gave an open invitation for bad spirits to enter the house. Babies' cradles should never be made of elder wood because that made it very easy for the fairies to steal the child and leave a changeling in its place.

DRIED ELDER FLOWERS

It is possible to dry elder flowers. They should be cut after three consecutive dry days once the dew has dried, but before mid-day when the sun may cause the flowers to wither slightly. Flowers which have just opened should be chosen. Remove the stems and spread them on racks over a stove or in an airing cupboard. They should become brittle within a few days. They are then ready to use. It is possible to buy commercially dried elder flowers.

ELDERFLOWER CHAMPAGNE

1 litre (2 pints) of elderflowers
725gm sugar (1½ lbs) sugar
Juice and rind of a lemon
2 tablespoons white vinegar
4 litres (8 pints) water
Place the elderflowers, sugar, lemon, vinegar and water into a non-metal container.
Leave for 24 hours.
Strain.
Bottle.

The champagne will be ready in about three weeks, but will be better if kept another three weeks, after which it begins to degenerate. Serve chilled.

ELDER TEA

Use an earthen-ware or china tea-pot because metal ones spoil the flavour. Warm the pot and place 3 teaspoons of flowers into the pot for every ½ litre (pint) of water. Either dried or fresh flowers may be used. Leave the tea to infuse for a few minutes, serve and sweeten to taste, preferably with honey rather than sugar, and drink without milk.

In the past elder-flower tea was used to treat colds and fevers.

ELDERFLOWER THIRST QUENCHER

Wash a few elderberry flowers, place them in a saucepan and pour boiling water on top of them.
Leave to cool.
Strain and add a little sugar, if required.

ELDER FLOWERS FOR A BEAUTIFUL SKIN

Elder flowers were used to cure spots and other skin blemishes by placing a handful of either fresh or dried elderflowers in a cup, covering them with boiling water. They were left to infuse for several hours and then the liquid was used to bathe the skin.

It is important to remember that all the old folk cures deteriorate quickly so the liquid should not be kept for more than a few days. It should be thrown out and some more made. It is easily done.

ELDERBERRIES TO CURE BURNS

The unripe, green elderberries were made into an ointment used to sooth burns. Lard 500gm (1 lb) was melted in a dish in the oven and used to cover as many green elderberries as possible. The dish holding the elderberries and melted lard was put back into the oven and left at a low temperature for two or three hours. More berries were added to the lard, which was then placed back in the oven for another two or three hours. After the second heating the mixture was cooled slightly and strained into small, warmed jars ready to spread on burns. I have never tried this. I do not like the idea of covering a burn with fat so intend to keep holding any burns I receive under cold water! I must admit I prefer the idea of making elderberry ointment to cure burns to another old folk cure, namely that of applying fresh cow manure!

FEVERFEW

Feverfew.

Feverfew grows to a height of about 60cm (2 feet). It has light yellow-green leaves and white daisy-type flowers from May to September. Feverfew is known locally as Mountain Daisy. It grows wild on waste ground, hedgerows, walls and in gardens, is very easy to grow and will seed itself once it becomes established. All the plant parts have a strong smell.

Feverfew was used to cure headaches, rheumatism, arthritis, lumbago and to cure fevers. It has been described as the asprin of the eighteenth century. It appears to work in the same way as asprin, affecting the size of blood vessels and suppressing inflammation. Medical research has found that it appears to keep the white blood cells, always found at the site of an infection, from making substances which damage the body.

Folk cures suggest that only a little feverfew is needed. It is not necessary to go out and eat a whole plant! All that is required is one large, or three small leaves. Place them in a sandwich, with perhaps a little honey. Eat a feverfew sandwich every day.

GARLIC

Garlic is particularly interesting as a folk remedy because it has gained the respect of the medical profession. It was widely used as a folk cure and commonly grown in Ireland until around the time of the First World War when it lost popularity.

Many people dislike the effect garlic has on the breath. Parsley is nature's breath freshener, it will reduce the smell if eaten after garlic. Today garlic perles are popular. When swallowed they pass into the stomach and hopefully quickly into the remainder of the digestive system without causing the tell-tale odour. The dosage is usually from one to three garlic perles swallowed with water three times a day.

In the past garlic was used as a cure all. A clove hung about the neck was believed to keep the devil at bay, it was eaten to cure stomach upsets, rubbed on sore, aching joints to treat rheumatism, heated and placed on corns to ease them, used as an antiseptic, squeezed against skin complaints and for heart disease. The Greek, Dioscorides, wrote thousands of years ago, 'Garlic doth clear the arteries.'

During the 1970s medical journals throughout the world published articles about the effect garlic has on arteries, blood cholesterol levels and high blood pressure. It would appear that the ancient healers, without knowing a single chemical fact about garlic had somehow stumbled upon its ability to help the health of the heart.

Garlic has been shown to lower blood cholesterol levels, prevent blood clots forming, raise low blood pressure and lower high blood pressure. It is not effective in treating high blood pressure caused by kidney disease, just the type with the following symptoms, lack of concentration, hypertension, dizziness and ringing in the ears.

Garlic has no ill effects. There are many potent modern drugs which may be used to treat heart disease but none of them can claim to be free from side effects.

HERB ROBERT

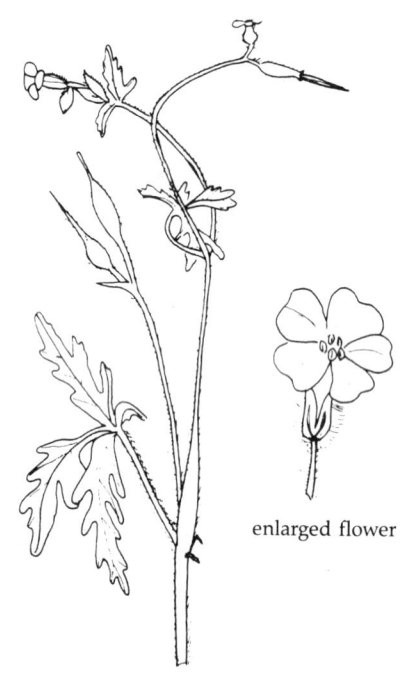

enlarged flower

Herb Robert is a very common plant, being found in woods, hedgebanks, stony places and in gardens where it is regarded as a weed. It grows up to a height of 45 cms and flowers from the end of April until October. The flowers are a reddish-violet colour, with long stalks. They usually grow in pairs and the petals have long "claws". The reddish stem is thick, juicy, forked and hairy. In fact, the whole plant is very hairy.

Herb Robert has been used medically for gout, enteritis, and diarrhoea. The plant stops bleeding if it is crushed against wounds and it can help cure sore mouths and tonsillitis if it is made into a decoction.

TO MAKE A DECOCTION OF HERB ROBERT

Place between one and three teaspoons of dried Herb Robert for each cup of water into a non-metal pot. Bring slowly to the boil and simmer for between fifteen and twenty minutes. Allow to cool and use as a gargle as soon as possible. The decoction should not be kept for more than twenty-four hours.

STINGING NETTLES

Stinging Nettle

Stinging Nettles have pale green flowers between May and September. They are very common in ditches, on the edges of woods, on waste ground and in hedgerows. They grow up to 1.5m (4ft 6ins) in height and have stings which can penetrate human skin causing nasty rashes. Nettle stings can be cured by rubbing them with dock leaves which are usually found growing near nettles. My grandfather used to say 'God puts the cure beside the curse!' When, as a child, I was stung by a nettle he would look for a dock leaf, rub it against the sting and say:-

'Docken in, docken out,
Take the sting of nettle out.'

In the past, believe it or not, nettles were used to make a very strong cloth, especially for tablecloths and sheets. They were also used to make fishermen's anchor ropes. A gargle made from the juice of nettles was thought to cure a fallen womb, although it is difficult to see how a gargle would help a womb! Drinking about 250cc (½ pint) of nettle juice was said to stop vomiting, spitting blood and haemorrhages. That sounds a bit more sensible because of nettles' Vitamin C content.

Crushed nettle leaves were placed against wounds to stop them bleeding and they were pounded with salt to cure the bites of mad dogs.

People suffering from whooping cough, phlegm in the lungs or shortness of breath swallowed nettle seeds mixed with honey. (Nettle seeds become ripe during the months of July and August when they may be gathered.)

Nettles are a good source of iron and of Vitamin C. Vitamin C helps the body to absorb iron. In the past Irish smallholders ate nettles three times during the spring to 'purify the blood'.

Tradition says that St. Columcille decided to mortify himself, and, no doubt his brother monks, during Lent, by eating nothing but a broth made from water, nettles and salt. He was asked by the cook if nothing else could go into the cooking pot. He replied with grim humour 'Nothing else will go into the broth except what comes out of the pot-stick'. The cook, with typical Irish logic, hollowed out his pot-stick and poured milk and oatmeal down it into the broth. The Saint had to abide by his own rules!

Stinging nettles are the only herb which may be found on the darkest night as well as in daylight! The poison in nettles, formic acid, is destroyed in the cooking. If nettles are grasped firmly they cannot sting but it does make life easier if gloves are donned before working with them.

The English and the Scots seem to have eaten as many nettles in the past as the Irish. Samuel Pepys wrote in his diary that he enjoyed a bowl of nettle porridge. The Scots and the Irish used nettles to make haggis and looked upon them as 'wild cabbage' or 'wild kale'. The plant we recognise as a 'cabbage' today is a comparative newcomer to Ireland.

In Scotland there are records of nettles being grown under glass as 'early kale'. Nettles were often referred to as 'greens' as in the following traditional verse:-

'Did you ever ate colcannon that's made from thickened cream.
With greens and scallions blended like a picture in your dream?
Did you ever take a forkful and dip it in the lake
Of the clover-flavoured butter which your mother used to make?'

COLCANNON (CHAMP)

Warm cooked potatoes
Cream or milk
Chopped scallions (also called spring onions)
Chopped, cooked nettles, (or cabbage)
Salt
Pepper
Butter
Cream the cooked potatoes with either cream or milk.
Add chopped scallions, and/or the nettles.
Mix.
Season to taste.
Serve by placing in a mound on the plate.
Make an indentation on the top of the mound and fill with butter.

NETTLES FOR BLOOD PURIFICATION

Nettles
Water
Collect fresh, green nettle tops.
Scald nettles by placing in a collander and pouring boiling water over them.
Place nettles in cooking pot.
Cover nettles with water.
Boil for 30 minutes.
A small amount of the infusion taken in the spring time was thought to purify the blood.

NETTLE CURE FOR CHEST AND THROAT COMPLAINTS

Boil nettles without salt.
Save the 'nettle water'.
Add enough honey to make a syrup.
Add a squeeze of lemon juice.
Take a spoonful whenever throat or cough is troublesome.

NETTLE SOUP

1¾ litres (3½ pints) young nettles
75g (3 oz) porridge oats
2 leeks (onions make a good substitute)
1 egg yolk
150 ml (¼ pint) cream
1½ litres (3 pints) stock
250 g (2 oz) butter
Salt and pepper

Fry the leeks and finely chopped nettles in the butter.
Add the stock, oats and seasonings.
Cook slowly for an hour.
Allow the soup to cool slightly.
Beat egg and cream together, add slowly to soup.
Reheat, but do not allow to boil.
There is an old saying:-

> 'A good soup boiled
> Is a good soup spoiled!'

NETTLE GRUEL

¾ litre (½ pint) chopped nettles
25g (1 oz) oatmeal
25g (1 oz) butter
½ litre (1 pint) milk or stock

Fry the oatmeal in the butter until browned.
Add stock, or milk and bring to boil.
Add finely chopped nettles and cook slowly for a few minutes.
Season with salt and pepper.
Mix in a little butter, or cream, or bacon fat.
Serve hot.
Nettles also taste good if they are cooked like spinach.

PRIMROSE

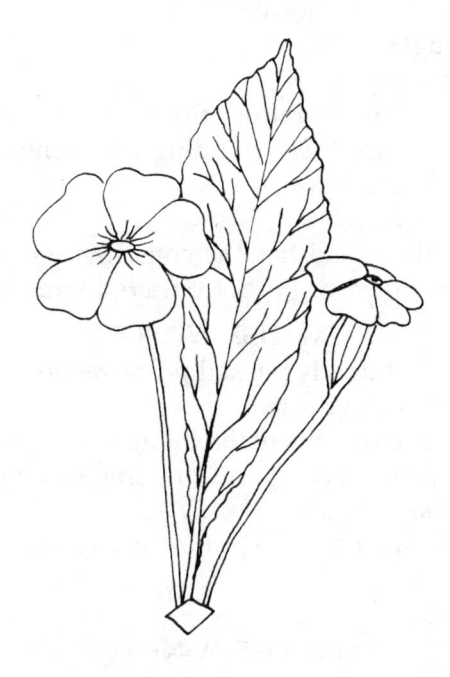

Primroses grow to a height of 20 cm, have pale lemon, five-petaled flowers, which appear in the Spring, and crinkly leaves which grow in a rosette. They are found in woods, hedgebanks and on grassy places. In some places they are an endangered species so should not be touched in the wild. It is possible to obtain primrose seed and to grow them in gardens.

In the past infusions of primrose flowers were used to cure headaches, insomnia and nervous conditions. The flowers act as a mild sedative. My son once ate six primroses and slept for the rest of the afternoon! They did not appear to have any ill effect as he was happy and in good form when he woke up. Candied primrose flowers make nice cake decorations.

PRIMROSE TEA

25g (1 oz) primrose blossoms
¾ litre (1½ pints) boiling water
Place the primrose blossoms in the water and leave for 30 minutes to infuse. Sweeten to taste and drink warm or cold.

PRIMROSE SYRUP

350 gm (12 oz) primrose flowers
200 gm (½ lb) sugar
½ litre (1 pint) boiling water
Make an infusion of the primrose flowers by covering them with boiling water and leave them standing for twenty-four hours.
Strain and discard the flowers.
Stir sugar into the infusion.
Boil gently until the liquid has the consistency of syrup.
Use to spread on bread or on hot buttered scones.

PRIMROSE WINE (1)

Use 1 litre (2 pints) of tightly packed primrose flowers for each 4½ litres (1 gallon) of boiling water.
Cover the primrose blossoms with boiling water and leave to soak for two or three days, stirring and pressing every day.
Strain into a fermenting jar.
Add 1½ kg (3 lb) sugar and 20 gm (¾ oz) yeast.
Ferment to finish.
Syphon and bottle.

PRIMROSE WINE (2)

4½ litres (1 gallon) primrose blossoms
4½ litres (1 gallon) boiling water
1½ kg sugar
1 tablespoon cold tea
1 orange
1 lemon
20g (¾ oz) yeast
Grate the rinds of the orange and the lemon.
Add the pith free rind and the juice of the orange and the lemon to the primrose flowers.
Add the sugar.
Add the cold tea.
Add the boiling water.
Allow to cool.
Add the yeast.
Leave to ferment for 48 hours.
Strain.
The wine is drinkable after three or four weeks. It may be bottled after two months. It will be improved if some spirits are added to it.

VIOLET

enlarged flower →

Violet.

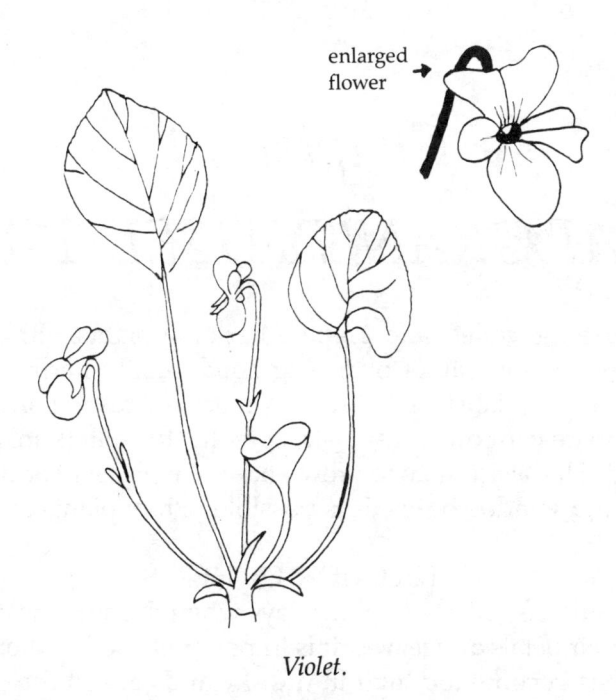

Violets are becoming rarer so they should not be disturbed in the wild. It is possible to buy violet plants or seeds and to grow them in gardens and use them in the old ways without harming the environment.

Dog violets are more common than sweet violets. Dog violets grow to a height of 20cm (15 ins) and are found blooming in woods and hedges from April to July. They vary in colour from blue to white.

The sweet violet is the violet with the famous perfume. It is rare in Ireland but may be found on hedgerows and wood edges. The colours also vary from blue to white.

Violet leaves and flowers have a high Vitamin C content. Both the leaves and the flowers taste good when added to salads. However it is not advisable to eat too many of them at one time because they have a slightly laxative effect! The flowers change colour in the presence of acids and alkalis so fruit salad will turn them red, as will lemon juice, while cream and milk will make them pale green.

Chapter 10
WHAT GRANNY USED TO DO

Granny used to collect and prepare her own plants, although the easiest and surest way of obtaining good quality herbs is to buy them from a specialist herbalist. It is more interesting and greater fun to prepare your own. Just make sure that the plants are properly identified. Herbs are easy to grow and make pleasant additions to gardens and windowboxes. It is possible to buy plants and seeds.

COLLECTION OF HERBS
Herbs should be collected on dry days when the sun has dried the dew off their petals and leaves. It is important to collect them before the sun has become too high in the sky and caused the plants to suffer slightly from lack of moisture.

DRYING HERBS
Plants are made from microscopic building blocks called cells. These cells begin to die as soon as they are cut off from their food supply and water. They must be spread out in a thin layer immediately, before the chemicals inside the cells begin to destroy them. There is an old saying 'Make sure plant material is killed before it has time to die!'

In this country herbs must be dried in artificial heat. Granny used the hot-press. She washed the herbs, shook the excess moisture off, threw out unwanted parts then spread the parts she wanted out on blotting paper. She also tied herbs in small bunches and hung then with their stems upwards on a line inside the hot-press.

Granny's clothes line used to look really peculiar on sunny days because she used to hang flowers, such as delphiniums and donkey's lug, to dry on it. She used these dried flowers in flower arrangements. She never dried herbs to be used as cures or in

cooking on the line. She said the sun took all the good out of them.
Dried flowers, stems and leaves become brittle. The drying time takes between a few days and a few weeks, depending on the species. If they are dried for too long they crumble into powder.
Dried herbs should be kept in tightly stoppered, glass containers. It is best to dry a new supply of herbs each year.

HERBAL BATHS

Granny used to enjoy simple herbal baths. She used to give a branch of rosemary to take into the bath with me and sometimes she mixed lavender with oatmeal, sewed the mixture into a muslim bag and hung it from the hotwater tap.

HERBAL VINEGARS

Steep a tablespoon of fresh or dried herbs in 250ml (¼ pint) of either wine or cider vinegar. Leave for at least 24 hours then strain and re-bottle.

HERBAL TEAS

Granny used to make delicious teas from many different herbs. She used raspberry leaves (she said this was very good for any woman who was going to have a baby), elder flowers, peppermint leaves, thyme, nettle leaves, lime flowers, rose petals and hips and wild strawberry leaves. She always used a china tea-pot, warmed it, then placed a heaped teaspoon of dried herb, or three teaspoons of fresh crushed herbs, for each cup in the pot. She added boiling water and allowed the tea to infuse for five minutes then strained it into a cup and sweetened it with honey.

Acknowledgements

I am very grateful to the following people who generously gave help and support. The Staff of the Ulster Folk and Transport Museum; Valerie Hall, Institute of Irish Studies, Queen's University Belfast; Liz Weir, Ulidia Resource Centre; Laurie Archibald, Industrial Research Centre, Lambeg, Co. Down; Dermot Magee; 'The Snug Restaurant', Enniskillen, County Fermanagh; Peter Mackenzie, 'The Bookworm', Bishop Street, Derry; Anna Crane and Peter Bailey, Dillons Bookshop; Alwyn Corrin, Fairfields Bookshop, Newtownards; 'Old Bushmills', Kirkpatrick Linron (Ballyclare) Ltd., Ernest Scott, local historian, Ballynure, Co.Antrim; Pat Cassidy, local historian Lisnaskea; County Fermanagh; Tom Porter, local historian Newcastle, County Down, who also gave kind permission to reproduce his poem 'Inblown Wrack'; Sheila Harrington, local historian, Bantry, County Cork; Margaret Graham and Frances Shaw, Banbridge, County Down. Thanks are also due to Norah Bates for information about her early years and for permission to reproduce her photograph of the family horse and cart, to Frank Downey, Ronnie Patton and other members of Banbridge Historical Society who read the manuscript, made valuable comment and provided help and encouragement; to Bobby Loan; Mrs Underwood; Michael Langley; Eamonn and Madelaine Coyle; Graham Millar; Robert Dunbar; Pat Meads; George Hall of Hallographics for his assistance in the production of the book; Ray McCullough of K. R. Graphics for the design of the cover; Romac Limited for the printing of the book and last, but not least to my family, especially my father, William Henry, for information concerning insurance of scutch mills and my husband for his unfailing patience in editing my manuscript.

Suggested Reading

'We Are Our Past', Doreen McBride, Adare Press 1990.
'Flower Power', Doreen McBride, Ulster Folk and Transport Museum 1987.
'Ulster Folk and Transport Museum Activity Guide', Doreen McBride, edited by Deidre Brown and Andrew Anderson, Longmans 1988.
'Ulster Farming', Jonathan Bell and Mervyn Watson, Ulster Folk and Transport Museum in conjunction with 'Farm Week' 1985.
'Farming in Ulster', Jonathan Bell and Mervyn Watson, Friars Bush Press 1988.
'Irish Farming', Jonathan Bell and Mervyn Watson, John Donald Publishers Ltd., 1986.
'Wild and Free', Cyril and Kit O Ceirin, The O'Brien Press 1986.
'Irish Country Cures', Patrick Logan, Appletree Press 1981.
'Herbal Delights', Mrs. C. F. Leyel, Faber and Faber 1937.
'An Irish Herbal', by John K'eogh, edited by Michael Scott, The Aquarian Press 1986.
'Gerald's Herbal', edited by Marcus Woodward, Bracken Books 1985.
'Herbs' Jack Harvey, Macdonald Optima 1988
'The Weaver's Grave', Seumas O'Kelly, The O'Brien Press, Dublin, 1984.
'Garlic', Paul Simmons, Thorsons Publishers Ltd., 1980.
'Old Wives Tales', Mary Chamberlain, Virago Press Ltd., 1981.
'Needlework Samplers of Northern Ireland', Heather M. Crawford, Allingham Press 1989. Available from Allingham Publishing, Sharon Lodge, Crawfordsburn, Northern Ireland.

Index

abscesses 24
arsenic 8
arteries 83
arthritis 82
artificial fertiliser 5
asprin 82
asthma 74
bacteria 26
barbed wire 31
barley 40
beet 11, 14, 15, 16
beetroot 65
besom 32
big gall 28
blackberry 65, 68, 69
blackberry and apple sweet 70
blackberry fool 70
blamange, carrageen 47
bleach green 22
blood pressure 83
blood purification 87
bracken 65
bronchitis 74
brush 31, 32
Bushmills Distillery 44
burns 24, 81
buttercup 72
cabbage 65
cake decorations 77
carbon dioxide 26, 41
Carleton, William 6
carrageen moss 45, 46, 47
carron oil 24
cells 92
champagne, elderflower 80
champ 87
chickweed 71, 72
chimney 31
chlorophyll 26, 27
cholesterol 83
chowes 18
cider vinegar 38
Clydesdale 59
clover 73
coffee 65
coffee, dandelion 76
colcannon 87
colds 73
constipation 24
Copper sulphate 6, 58
cough 74
cows 28
crab apple 35-39, 65
dandelion 8, 65, 75-76
coffee 76
diarrhoea 73, 84
distillation 43
dog rose 77-78
Druid 35
dulaman 45

dulse 45, 47, 48
dunghill 6, 7
dyes, cudbear 63
logwood 62
plant 62-66
whin 32
earwig 8
elder 79, 80, 81
champagne 80
dried flowers 80
treatment for burns 81
treatment for skin 81
enteritis 84
fairies 35
feet, cure for smelly 51
fencing 30
fermentation 41, 43
fertiliser 5, 6, 8, 26, 29, 30, 49
feverfew 82
flax 9, 10, 17, 18, 19
flax dam 14
fodder 27, 28, 29
foxgloves 62
furze, see whins
gatin 16, 17
garlic 83
gorse, see whins
gout 84
heartburn 33
headaches 82, 89
heart disease 83
hedging 27
herb 92
herb robert 84
herbal baths 93
tea 93
vinegar 93
horse 27
hovel 17
hydrangea 63
hypertension 83
insomnia 89
iron 86
jelly carageen 47
crab apple 38
crab apple and blackberry 39
crab apple and rose hip 39
kelp 53, 54, 55
kidney 75, 76
Kirkpatrick Linron (Ballyclare) Ltd 24
kitchen 45
Lammas Fair 45
laryngitis 74
laver 45
laxative 91
lazy bed 56
lesser celandine 72
lichen 63

linen 9, 10, 11, 12, 13, 18, 19, 22, 24
linen mill 22, 24
linen threads 9
linron 24
linseed oil 24, 25
linoleum 24
lint dam 14
logwood 62
loom 19
lumbago 82
meadow sweet 62
manure 5, 6, 30, 49, 51
milk 30
mordant 62, 64, 65, 66
mouth 24, 84
mousse, apple and blackberry 39
National Health Service 67, 77
nervous conditions 89
nettle 7, 65, 85
champ 87
colcannon, see champ
gruel 88
soup 88
nitrates 7
nitrogen bacteria 26
oare 45
oatmeal 93
Ocean Insurance Company 18
onions 7, 62, 65
phlegm 86
pigments 62-63
piles 72
pile wort, see lesser celandine
plant succession 10
plots 60
plough 61
potato 57-61
blight 58
clamp 61
harvest 61
skins 28, 43
poteen 40-44
kettle 43
men 42
residue 44
primrose 89-90
syrup 90
tea 90
wine 90
privet 65
putty 24, 25
ragwort 65
raspberry 93
ray 17
retting 14, 15
rick 17, 54, 55
rippling 11
rippling comb 11, 14

rheumatism 82, 83
rheumatic joints 74
roads 32
rousel 57
rose (dog) 77-78
Saint Brigid 36
salad, chickweed 71
clover 73
dandelion 76
scurvy 71
scutch mill 17, 18
sea weed 45 - 55
sedative 89
shamrock 73
skin 74, 81, 83
sleigh 17
sloke 45
spade 58
spots 24
stomach, 73, 83
syrup, dandelion 76
primrose 90
rose hip 78
tattie howking 61
tea, clover 73
elder 81
lime 93
peppermint 93
primrose 89
raspberry 93
rose hip 78
rose petal 93
thyme 93
throat 24, 87
toilet 6
tonsillitis 84
Trinity 73
tumour 24
urine 7, 63, 64
vegetable, chickweed 72
dandelion 76
dulse 48
verjuice 38
violet 91
Vitamin C 68 71, 77, 86, 91
watch tower 19
weedkiller 8
well 32
whins 26-34, 65
wine, whin 33-34
whiskey 44
whooping cough 86
womb 86
worms 33
wounds 38
wrack 49, 51, 52, 53, 55
beds 53
road 51
wounds 38
yeast 40, 90